MEASURE FOR MEASURE

MEASURE FOR MEASURE

William Shakespeare

Edited by
CEDRIC WATTS

WORDSWORTH CLASSICS

In loving memory of
MICHAEL TRAYLER
the founder of Wordsworth Editions

3

Readers who are interested in other titles from
Wordsworth Editions are invited to visit our website at
www.wordsworth-editions.com

For our latest list and a full mail-order service, contact
Bibliophile Books, 5 Thomas Road, London E14 7BN
TEL: +44 (0)20 7515 9222 FAX: +44 (0)20 7538 4115
E-MAIL: orders@bibliophilebooks.com

Published by Wordsworth Editions Limited
8B East Street, Ware, Hertfordshire SG12 9HJ

ISBN 978 1 85326 251 7

Text © Wordsworth Editions Limited 2005
Introduction, notes and all other editorial matter
© Cedric Watts, 2005

This newly-edited volume was first published in 2005.

Typeset in Great Britain by Antony Gray
Printed and bound by Clays Ltd, St Ives plc

CONTENTS

GENERAL INTRODUCTION

In the new Wordsworth Classics' Shakespeare Series, the inaugural
volumes, *Romeo and Juliet*, *The Merchant of Venice* and *Henry V*,
have been followed by *The Taming of the Shrew*, *A Midsummer
Night's Dream*, *Much Ado about Nothing*, *Julius Cæsar*, *Hamlet*,
Twelfth Night, *Measure for Measure*, *Othello*, *King Lear*, *The Winter's
Tale* and *The Tempest*. Previously, the Wordsworth Shakespeare
volumes often adopted, by arrangement, an earlier Cambridge
University Press text. The new series, however, consists of fresh
editions specially commissioned for Wordsworth Classics. Each
play in this emergent Shakespeare Series is accompanied by a
standard apparatus, including an introduction, explanatory notes
and a glossary. The textual editing takes account of recent
scholarship, while giving the material a careful reappraisal. The
apparatus is, however, concise rather than elaborate. We hope
that the resultant volumes prove to be handy, reliable and helpful.
Above all, we hope that, from Shakespeare's works, readers will
derive pleasure, wisdom, provocation, challenges, and insights:
insights into his culture and ours, and into the era of civilisation
to which his writings have made (and continue to make) such
potently influential contributions. Shakespeare's eloquence will,
undoubtedly, re-echo 'in states unborn and accents yet unknown'.

CEDRIC WATTS
Series Editor

INTRODUCTION

Thus . . . at the close our feeling is neither of simple joy nor pain; we are excited, fascinated, perplexed, for the issues raised preclude a completely satisfactory outcome, even when, as in . . . *Measure for Measure*, the complications are outwardly adjusted in the fifth act.

(F. S. Boas.)[1]

Measure for Measure . . . also has its 'deeply satisfying', 'astonishing, wondrous aspects' of the kind summed up in the immortal 'Goody-Goody' (by Johnny Mercer and Matt Malneck):

> Hooray and hallelujah!
> You had it comin' to ya!

(Harriett Hawkins.) [2]

Measure for Measure is one of the best of Shakespeare's plays, though it has not always received the appreciation it deserves. For instance, while some people have found its sexual explorations engaging, others have found them disgusting. It has often been termed 'a problem play', and this categorisation is partly negative and partly positive. To people who hold conventional ideas of comedy, *Measure for Measure* is generically problematic. You can soon see why. Although its mainly positive ending seems to locate it in the *genre* or category of comedy, the play contains a remarkable amount of grim, harsh, cynical and painful material, and by Act 3 it summons the ominous intensity of a tragedy. (Sir Edmund Chambers declared this a 'bitter and cynical' work which 'drags the honour of womanhood in the dust'; Algernon

Swinburne believed that it belonged to a small group of 'tragedies docked of their natural end'.[3]) On the other hand, the less conventional your generic notions, the more enjoyable is *Measure for Measure*. Then you can appreciate it as 'a problem play' in the positive sense: as a play which explores important problems; and here the exploration is intelligent, eloquent and moving. In this case, they are interlinked problems of politics, religion and morality. They were important in Shakespeare's time, and they remain so today.

One political and judicial problem is that of effecting the best compromise between individual liberty and social order. Another is that of effecting the best middle course, in sexual morality, between the extreme of decadent license, on one side, and of repressive severity, on the other. Should justice err on the side of sternness or on that of lenience? Is a death-sentence ever justifiable? Yet another problem is that of establishing government which is knowledgeably effective but not demeaningly manipulative. Then there are problems of religion: should religious principles guide the state, or should the state's principles be flexible and largely secular? And, for every individual, there are the questions about death: is it a dreamless sleep from which we never wake, or is it the gateway to an afterlife of bliss or of purgatorial suffering or of eternal damnation?

The excellence of *Measure for Measure* lies largely in the panache with which all these problems are fluently interlinked and vividly rendered. We enter no abstract debate but a social arena in which credible characters deliberate, jest, quarrel, suffer and learn. There's the Duke, undertaking a controlled experiment with morality, justice, and human lives: but can he maintain his control? And isn't he more fallible than he realises? There's the ironically-named Angelo, his appointed deputy, striving to uphold a puritanical mandate, but discovering within himself depths of repressed desire which change him into a sadistic would-be rapist. There's Isabella, whose virtue is part of her appeal for Angelo, and who is determined not to sacrifice her virginity to save her brother's life. Is she heroic, or is she seeking to evade full self-recognition? Then there's Claudio, the brother, sentenced to die for impregnating his fiancée outside holy wedlock, now striving for life, now acquiescing in death, now again seeking desperately to live. In Act 3, scene 1, consider the sequence whereby he is first comforted by the Duke disguised as a friar, then learns from Isabella of the possibility that her virginity might buy his life, and quarrels desperately with her until impasse is reached. That sequence is one of the most powerful ever written for the theatre, and, as it gathers momentum, it surges with passionate vitality.

See how it's done. In that scene, Claudio tells the 'Friar-Duke' that he is prepared to die, while hoping for life. The Friar-Duke replies:

> Be absolute for death: either death or life
> Shall thereby be the sweeter. Reason thus with life:
> If I do lost thee, I do lost a thing
> That none but fools would keep: a breath thou art,
> Servile to all the skyey influences
> That dost this habitation, where thou keep'st,
> Hourly afflict. Merely, thou art Death's fool;
> For him thou labour'st by thy flight to shun,
> And yet run'st toward him still.

And so the 'friar' continues: confident, reassuring, almost tran- quillising; indeed, as he proceeds with his illustrations of the vanity of life and the restfulness of death, his very tone seems to induce calmness. It's a paradoxical speech from a supposed friar, for he says nothing about Heaven, Hell and Purgatory. His insistence on death as a dreamless sleep is pagan, indeed Epicurean, rather than Christian. Nevertheless, it serves its apparent function of reconciling young Claudio to the prospect of his execution.

Then Claudio's sister, Isabella, arrives, and, very reluctantly, reveals that there's a chance he may live, but a chance she is sure he will not accept. He tells her that he is not afraid to die; but his curiosity is aroused, and gradually she reveals Angelo's foul offer: Claudio will live if Isabella sacrifices her virginity to Angelo. 'Thou shalt not do't', Claudio says. Isabella responds:

> O, were it but my life,
> I'd throw it down for your deliverance
> As frankly as a pin.

'Thanks, dear Isabel', responds Claudio. Isabel, in whom tact is not prominent, says: 'Be ready, Claudio, for your death tomorrow.' But he has been quietly brooding on Angelo's offer, and reflects that lust is, at worst, surely the least of the seven deadly sins. Isabella is disconcerted, but Claudio pursues the matter:

> If it were damnable, he being so wise,
> Why would he for the momentary trick
> Be pérdurably fined? O Isabel!

In other words, if it is a deadly sin, why would the wise Angelo risk eternal damnation for a brief sexual 'trick', a fleeting orgasm? Isabella registers increasing alarm as Claudio gradually finds Angelo's offer tempting. 'Death is a fearful thing', says Claudio; 'And shamèd life a hateful', she responds. This response provokes from him one of the finest speeches in literature: it's like a great aria in an opera. He begins:

> Ay, but to die, and go we know not where;
> To lie in cold obstruction, and to rot;
> This sensible warm motion to become
> A kneaded clod; and the delighted spirit
> To bathe in fiery floods, or to reside
> In thrilling regions of thick-ribbèd ice;
> To be imprisoned in the viewless winds,
> And blown with restless violence round about
> The pendent world; or to be worse than worst
> Of those that lawless and incertain thoughts
> Imagine howling: 'tis too horrible!

With vivid and accelerating eloquence, he invokes this surrealistic, phantasmagoric vista of post-mortal existence: the warm body becoming a mere clod of kneadable clay, the delectable spirit forced to experience not delights but horrors as it is immersed in fire, or is fixed in chilling regions of thickly-gnarled ice, or is blown round and round the world in the invisible winds, or even becomes worse than worst of those who (we may illicitly and speculatively imagine) howl in Purgatory: compared with that, the most wretched of living existences seems a Paradise. No wonder he concludes: 'Sweet sister, let me live!'. After all, if she sacrifices her virginity to save a brother's life, isn't that an act of virtue, not a sin?

Isabella is horrified, and in a passionately vituperative outburst cries:

> O you beast!
> O faithless coward, O dishonest wretch!
> Wilt thou be made a man out of my vice?
> Is't not a kind of incest, to take life
> From thine own sister's shame?

She reasons that if, as a result of her act of copulation, her brother gained life anew, it would be as if she had given birth to a brother, thus making the sexual act retrospectively incestuous. Her fury increases; she sweeps aside his protestation, declaring it's best that he die quickly; and, as matters thus reach an impasse, the Friar-Duke suddenly steps forward to guide matters on their erratic course towards constructive resolution. But, until then, the sequence that we have witnessed has superbly linked the abstract, the philosophical and the theological to the concrete, material and carnal. The argument about the nature of death has been passionately and intimately combined with an argument about the ethics of submitting to sexual blackmail if it promises to save a life (a promise which may not be kept). This is intelligent drama at its best, registering the cost in individual emotions of ideological confusion and moral conflict. The psychological realism, as Claudio's burgeoning anxiety to live elicits Isabella's growing indignation and horror, is as acute as you could find in Ibsen or Strindberg, while the ranges of imagery and rhythm offer the vistas and the momentum that only great verse-drama can command.

By the contrast between the Friar-Duke's incantatory speech on death as sleep and Claudio's impetuously intense speech on death as gateway to possible horror, we have been challenged to inspect our own views on death and, thereby (as Claudio shows), on the nature and value of life itself. As we listen to the argument between Isabella and her brother, our sympathies are pulled to and fro. Part of us sides with Claudio: of course, to anyone faced with execution, the thought that life might be granted in return for a few minutes of sexual gratification may make the carnal price seem trivial. But part of us surely sides with Isabella, too. She was embarking on the dedicated career of a nun in a convent; so her virginity has immense symbolic value, because a nun becomes the bride of Christ. Why should she destroy the symbol of spiritual purity to prolong the life of a brother who, if he had exercised sexual restraint himself, would not now be under sentence of death? Why should she, an intelligently independent woman, submit to a sadistic male extortioner?

Thus the play does not simply present for contemplation a set of elegantly-combined problems; it shows how they mesh with the lives of individuals; and, as we observe and become involved with the characters, so those problems mesh with our experience and our inner lives. Of course, it is one thing to experience dilemmas; it is another thing to see how such dilemmas are solved. One of the most controversial features of the play is the rôle of the apparent problem-solver, the Friar-Duke himself. In a very influential essay of 1930, G. Wilson Knight challenged the widespread view that *Measure for Measure* was morbid, cynical and inwardly divided.[4] Far from being divided, it was (he claimed) a splendid unity, and a morally magnificent Duke presided over it.

> Much has been said about the difficulties of *Measure for Measure*. But, in truth, no play of Shakespeare shows more thoughtful care, more deliberate purpose, more consummate skill in structural technique, and, finally, more penetrating ethical and psychological insight. None shows a more exquisitely inwoven pattern.[5]

The basis of that pattern, Knight asserts, is 'the sublime strangeness and unreason of Jesus' teaching'; so the play 'must be read . . . as a parable': it 'tends towards allegory or symbolism'. 'Isabella stands for sainted purity, Angelo for Pharasaical righteousness, the Duke for a psychologically sound and enlightened ethic.' Indeed, the Duke is 'automatically comparable with Divinity'. A stern ethic is tested, human fallibility is revealed, and finally the Christian 'moral of love' is vindicated.

Wilson Knight's challenging essay had a great influence on subsequent critics and directors; notably, on F. R. Leavis, Henri Fluchère, Roy Battenhouse, Nevill Coghill and Raymond Raikes. A radio production by Raikes used various devices (including an echo-chamber and angelic choirs) to suggest that the Duke was God in disguise, while Lucio, speaking in cynical and sinister tones, was evidently a relative of Lucifer, the eternal adversary.[6] In turn, Wilson Knight's polemical interpretation attracted a variety of counter-attacks, of which the most adroitly penetrating and theologically insolent was A. D. Nuttall's. He saw the play as jagged and awkward, displaying technical neatness and metaphysical disorder: it resembled 'a minuet worked out in a sequence of violent discords'. We should recognise 'that Angelo is, on a modest computation . . . worth about six Dukes'. You'll recall that, in response to pleas for mercy from Escalus and Isabella, Angelo said that the law must be upheld; society needs it. Nuttall argues that it is Angelo's stern ethic which, in practice, we do and should support. The play offers a 'tender' Christian ethic: 'No man who is not himself perfect has the right to judge a fellow creature. Man can only forgive . . . '. It also offers a related 'tender' but non-Christian ethic: 'anybody without a bit of generous vice in him isn't properly human'; like the former, this advises us to forgive. Against these, the play offers a 'tough' ethic: '*of course* none of us is perfect but *of course* we must judge':

> Now, do we really think that because none of us is perfect so no one should judge – that is, in hard terms, there should be no law-courts, no penal system, no juries, no police? Certainly judges are imperfect, but equally certainly it is a job that someone has to do.[7]

Admittedly, continues Nuttall, Angelo's ethic naturally lacks the tender ethic's power to 'give us warm feelings', but it is practical, it is supported by Shakespeare's presentation of the foul brothel-world, and it is ours. In contrast, the Duke (whom Wilson Knight saw virtually as God walking the earth) is ethically irresponsible. Having ruled so slackly that corruption is rife, he gives Angelo the task of reforming the state; and when, as a consequence, the laws are sternly enforced, the Duke 'proceeds by an orgy of clemency at the close to undo all the good achieved'. The Duke is inconsistent in seeking simultaneously to test Angelo and to improve the administration of justice. If he has doubts about Angelo's probity (as he has), he should not entrust him with this important task.

You may begin to suspect that if a critic regards a text as valuable, egotism (and, no doubt, higher motives) will tempt him or her to offer an interpretation which implies that the text has astutely succeeded in adopting his or her own prejudices (or principles).

Just as a Christian commentator is likely to emphasise the Christian elements of *Measure for Measure*, and as a sceptical commentator is likely to commend its impious elements, so a politically right-wing critic is likely to commend conservative aspects of the text (e.g. by applauding the wisdom of the Duke), and a politically left-wing critic is likely to commend rebellious aspects (e.g. by treating sympathetically Lucio and Pompey). Similarly, feminists may, understandably, magnify the importance and merit of Isabella, and may detect complicity with a nasty Angelo in any male critic who deems her neurotic. By its volatile presentation of characters and problems, by its meshwork of ironies and paradoxes, *Measure for Measure* seems designed to make us wrangle.[8]

Writing as a 'cultural materialist', Jonathan Dollimore has claimed that *Measure for Measure* offers an object-lesson in suspect modes of social control: we learn from it how Machiavellian the state can be.

> By means of the Duke's personal intervention and integrity, authoritarian reaction is put into abeyance but not discredited: the corrupt deputy is unmasked but no law is repealed and the mercy exercised remains the prerogative of the same ruler who initiated reaction . . . What Foucault has said of sexuality in the nineteenth and twentieth centuries seems appropriate also to sexuality as a sub-category of sin in earlier periods: it *appears* to be that which power is afraid of but in actuality is that which power works through. Sin, especially when internalised as guilt, has produced the subjects of authority as surely as any ideology.[8]

Dollimore claims that even those characters who seem to offer resistance to authority actually endorse it. (Pompey, we recall, readily serves as the executioner's assistant; Lucio struts and postures as a loyal foe to subversion when supporting Angelo and Escalus against the 'friar'.) Furthermore, 'the prostitutes, the most exploited group in the society which the play represents, are absent from it': 'they have no voice, no presence'.

One theme of such accounts as Nuttall's and Dollimore's, we may reflect, has its keynote in Elbow's repeated confusion of 'respected' and 'suspected' (2.1.152–70): the once-respected Duke has become suspected, and the text is valued not for the ducal process which Wilson Knight, F. R. Leavis and others found so humane, but for its illustrations of the devious ways by which authority controls and represses humanity. Feminist discussions of the play also vary considerably in their view of authority and of Isabella's relationship to it. In *Shakespeare and the Nature of Women*, Juliet Dusinberre claimed that Shakespeare aided the cause of women by popularising the Protestant reformers' hostility to monasticism and their advocacy of the married state. Thus, Isabella learns that the true testing-ground for virtue is the world of practical endeavour and eventual marriage, rather than the maidenly seclusion of the cloister.[9] In *Still Harping on Daughters*, however, Lisa Jardine argued that Isabella fails to conform to conventional stereotypes of the submissive female:

> Shakespeare's Isabella is belittled by the stereotypes to whom [*sic*] she so flagrantly refuses to match up. Her stature is diminished, her virtue is placed in question . . . Isabella's crude accusation of 'incest', and the claim that her enforced sex would 'make a man' of Claudio does nothing to elevate her in the audience's eyes.[10]

Of course, one consequence of the progress of feminism during the second half of the twentieth century was that Isabella's silence in the last few minutes of the play gained fresh scrutiny. At 5.1.499-500, the Duke clearly makes a proposal of marriage to her: 'and, for your lovely sake, / Give me your hand, and say you will be mine'. Yet Isabella utters not a word of response, even though it would have been so easy for the playwright to grant her an acquiescent pentameter (such as: 'Dear Lord, I gladly pledge myself your own.'). Traditionally, stage productions employed acquiescent body-language to fill her silence: she would accept the Duke's hand gladly, smiling and moving close to him. Perhaps this is what Shakespeare intended. After all, the Duke, having made his marital intention clear, continues to dispense justice in an unruffled manner, so, textually, there is nothing to indicate that he receives a rebuff from her; and, in the closing moments, he returns in seemingly-genial tones to the matter of marriage:

> Dear Isabel,
> I have a motion much imports your good;
> Whereto if you'll a willing ear incline,
> What's mine is yours, and what is yours is mine.

It is easy to assume that she departs arm-in-arm with him, there being no discordant note in the closing couplet which ensues. We know that she has hitherto gladly co-operated with the Friar-Duke's schemes. Nevertheless, some stage productions have exploited her silence by letting it be disruptive of the Duke's climactic endeavour to resolve events harmoniously. In performances at Stratford-upon-Avon in 1970, the director, John Barton, arranged for Isabella to be left alone on stage at the end, gazing at the audience in shocked bewilderment. Similarly, when Jonathan Miller directed the play (at the National Theatre in 1973 and at Greenwich in 1975), Isabella clearly rejected the Duke, recoiling in horror from his proposal. A reviewer reported:

> The Duke . . . , who has pimped for Mariana, responds to [Isabella's] spiritual drabness which has eluded his temporal jurisdiction, and the play ends with his summary dismissal of his underlings, so that he, like Angelo, can proposition Isabella. It is like a gloomy Thurberesque variant on the boss and secretary routine: the ugly stenographer in novitiate's garb retreating in horrified silence from the middle-aged executive in monkish garb.[11]

Such an ending, it can be argued, is true to Isabella's character, for she had sought initially to retreat from the world of men to the world of the cloister, and she has recently undergone bruising encounters with masculine lust, cruelty, deception and hypocrisy. If she rejects the Duke's proposal, this calls in question his general air of patronising control and his assumption that he knows what is right for everybody else. Even more: her action discloses the extent to which woman have served as auxiliaries in a political arena dominated by men. Subsequently in the theatre, therefore, *Measure for Measure* has become one of the most interestingly unpredictable of Shakespeare's plays. Will a new Isabella gladly accept the Duke, thus apparently endorsing his ways and increasing the sense of comedic closure; or will she reject him, thus emphasising her own recalcitrance and thereby completing the sequence of subversive features in the plot? Or will other options for her be dramatised?

A particularly engaging and animating feature of *Measure for Measure* is that our attitudes to numerous characters are curiously variable: now we sympathise with a given character, and now we feel hostile to the same character. The Duke, Angelo, Isabella and Claudio can all divide our feelings, but so can lesser figures. Escalus seems initially wise and tolerant, but even he reaches the point where he demands that innocent people be hauled off to jail and tortured on the rack until their joints are torn apart. The Provost, too, appears to be a very civilised prison-governor, until we notice that his idea of moral therapy is 'very oft' to awaken Barnardine and present him with a false warrant for his immediate execution. As for Barnardine, the dissolute prisoner: what is his main function? Is it to make Claudio and Angelo seem better by contrast, for, unlike him, they scrutinise their consciences; or to make the Duke seem worse, because the Duke is initially keen to have the convict's head chopped off; or to make the Duke seem better, as he eventually pardons Barnardine and assures him of counselling; or is it to be an incarnate argument against capital punishment, since, although Barnardine is a drunken rogue, his truculent defiance elicits our sympathies? Then there is Lucio. Certainly, this 'gentleman' delights in slander, frequents a brothel, and selfishly denies paternity of his illegitimate child. Nevertheless, it is the same character whose description of Juliet's pregnancy, offsetting the negative views from Claudio and the Friar-Duke (who see it as evidence of license and sin), is richly positive in its natural imagery:

> Your brother and his lover have embraced:
> As those that feed grow full, as blossoming time
> That from the seedness the bare fallow brings
> To teeming foison, even so her plenteous womb
> Expresseth his full tilth and husbandry.

It is Lucio, too, whose urging impels Isabella to greater eloquence when she flags in defending Claudio at her first interview with Angelo. If we look further down the social scale, we find that Abhorson, the executioner, is not quite as abhorrent as his name suggests: he takes pride in his vocation, complaining that if he accepts Pompey as an assistant, the presence of this pimp will discredit it. Pompey, in turn, is no mere provider of 'comic relief', for his rôle as recidivist adds to the debate about justice and mercy, while his jaunty defence of the carnal forms part of the problem of sexuality and the law. 'Does your Worship mean to geld and splay all the youth of the city?', he asks Escalus; and, when Escalus replies 'No, Pompey', he declares:

> Truly, sir, in my poor opinion, they will to't then. If your Worship will take order for the drabs and the knaves, you need not to fear the bawds.

In other words, if you don't neuter young people, they'll find a way of fornicating; and, if the law could repress the whores and their customers, pimps would present no problem. Even when we then consider Mistress Overdone, that much-married brothel-keeper, we find something to engage as well as to deride: she worries like any respectable business-woman at the prospect of redundancy, and it is she who has nursed Lucio's rejected infant. In short, *Measure for Measure* looks like an ambitious and exuberant experiment in the depiction of characters who are either ambiguous or, at least, credibly mixed in nature.[12] This makes it perilous for critics (since it exposes their prejudices), but tempting for directors and rewarding for actors.

Measure for Measure is certainly instructive, but it is designed to entertain. As we read or watch the play, our ethical judgements are sometimes supported and sometimes opposed by our aesthetic judgements. An argument of which we disapprove ethically may be expressed in ways that are aesthetically pleasing. Our moral hopes sometime clash with our desire for imaginative excitement. One example is this: morally, we probably hope that Claudio will not be executed, but part of us relishes the dramatic turmoil that would ensue if he were to be. Another is that Angelo's corruption is both deplorable and gratifying (suspense is generated, and the biter is bitten). Even though we may already be familiar with the play's outcome, a good stage or screen production will not only renew our attention to the immediate but will also thereby regenerate our sense of alternative predictive sequences, that is, of different conceivable courses for the unfolding action. Repeatedly we envisage the beckoning but neglected options We may experience a marked contrast between the play as imagined during our reading of the text and the play as it unfolds before us in performance. The music usually becomes more notable and emotive; grimace and gesture may make the comedy funnier; innovative sets and costumes may boldly link the fictional past with the real present. And we recognise that no production is ever neutral. The settings, the tones and styles of the characters, and the inter-actions between them, may emphasise right-wing rather than left-wing political implications, or sceptical rather than religious commendations; while the sense of aesthetic richness may subvert those political and religious aspects.

Metaphysically, morally, politically and aesthetically, *Measure for Measure* remains richly ambiguous. It artfully solicits a diversity of interpretations. The play cogently asks the questions, leaving us to find the answers. That quest could be lengthy but fulfilling.

NOTES TO THE INTRODUCTION

1 F. S. Boas: *Shakspere and His Predecessors* (London: Murray 1896), p. 345. Boas proposed that four plays by Shakespeare, *Hamlet*, *Troilus and Cressida*, *All's Well That Ends Well* and *Measure for Measure*, should be termed 'the problem-plays'. The term (usually without the hyphen) was widely adopted. The last three plays were sometimes also designated 'the problem comedies' or 'the dark comedies'.

2 Harriett Hawkins: *Measure for Measure* (Brighton: Harvester, 1987), pp. 118–19.

3 Chambers: *Encyclopaedia Britannica* (14th edition), Vol. 20, p. 446. Swinburne: *A Study of Shakespeare* (London: Chatto & Windus, 1880), p. 194. Among the critics who emphasised the 'dark' or 'morbid' aspects of the play were S. T. Coleridge, Sir Arthur Quiller-Couch, John Dover Wilson, Caroline Spurgeon, Una Ellis-Fermor and Theodore Spencer. Coleridge, for example, declared the comic parts 'disgusting', the tragic parts 'horrible'.

4 G. Wilson Knight: '*Measure for Measure* and the Gospels' in *The Wheel of Fire* (London: Oxford University Press, 1930), pp. 80–106.

5 Wilson Knight, p. 106.

6 In that radio production (27 March 1955), the Christian interpretation was aided by excisions from the text, notably of passages which present Lucio as sympathetic rather than cynical.

7 A. D. Nuttall: 'Measure for Measure: Quid Pro Quo?': *Shakespeare Studies* 4 (1968), p. 242.

8 The main source of *Measure for Measure* was George Whetstone's play, *Promos and Cassandra* (first printed in 1579). Shakespeare, while deriving many elements from Whetstone, has markedly intensified the dramatic conflicts by means of his greater eloquence and his intelligence in accentuating the temperamental and ethical contrasts. (By making the

heroine a novitiate, for instance, Shakespeare intensifies her dilemma; and, by making both Angelo and Lucio betrayers of women, he extends the network of comparisons.)

8   Jonathan Dollimore: 'Transgression and Surveillance in *Measure for Measure*' in *Political Shakespeare: New Essays in Cultural Materialism*, ed. Jonathan Dollimore and Alan Sinfield (Manchester: Manchester University Press, 1985), pp. 83 and 85. (Cultural materialists claimed Karl Marx as a mentor.) Dollimore cites the theories of Michel Foucault, famed for his *Histoire de la sexualité* (eventually 3 vols., 1976, 1984, 1984, translated as *The History of Sexuality*, 1979, 1986, 1988). Foucault developed the notion that authority generates apparent resistance to itself in order to strengthen itself. Critics of Foucault's paradox pointed out that real revolutions had sometimes occurred.

9   Juliet Dusinberre: *Shakespeare and the Nature of Women* (London: Macmillan, 1975; rpt., 1985), p. 42. Germaine Greer also saw Shakespeare as progressive: 'He projected the ideal of the monogamous heterosexual couple so luminously [in his writings] that they irradiate our notions . . . to this day.' See her *Shakespeare* (Oxford: Oxford University Press. 1986), p. 124.

10 Lisa Jardine: *Still Harping on Daughters* (Brighton: Harvester, 1983), pp. 191–2.

11 Review by Craig Raine of Miller's 1975 Greenwich Theatre production (*New Statesman*, Vol. 90, 22 August 1975, p. 230).

12 Bertolt Brecht, widely regarded as a Marxist dramatist, was encouraged by the example of Shakespearian drama to develop his theory of *Verfremdungseffekten* (Alienation Devices), which includes, for instance, the recommendation that a leading character should appear to the audience as partly attractive and partly repulsive. Between 1931 and 1934 Brecht adapted *Measure for Measure* as *Die Rundköpfe und die Spitzköpfe* (*Round Heads and Pointed Heads*), an allegory in which the Duke becomes a Viceroy who represents capitalism, while Angelo becomes Angelo Iberin, a deputy who represents Adolf Hitler.

FURTHER READING
(in chronological order)

F. S. Boas: *Shakspere and His Predecessors*. London: Murray, 1896.

G. Wilson Knight: *The Wheel of Fire*. London: Oxford University Press, 1930.

W. W. Lawrence: *Shakespeare's Problem Comedies*. New York: Macmillan, 1931.

E. M. W. Tillyard: *Shakespeare's Problem Plays*. London: Chatto & Windus, 1950.

Narrative and Dramatic Sources of Shakespeare, Vol. 2, ed. Geoffrey Bullough. London: Routledge & Kegan Paul, 1958.

Discussions of Shakespeare's Problem Comedies, ed. Robert Ornstein. Boston, Mass.: D. C. Heath, 1961.

Ernest Schanzer: *The Problem Plays of Shakespeare: A Study of 'Julius Cæsar', 'Measure for Measure', 'Antony and Cleopatra'*. London: Routledge & Kegan Paul, 1963.

Twentieth Century Interpretations of 'Measure for Measure': A Collection of Critical Essays, ed. George L. Geckle. Englewood Cliffs, N. J.: Prentice-Hall, 1970.

Shakespeare: 'Measure for Measure': A Casebook, ed. C. K. Stead. Basingstoke and London: Macmillan, 1971

Juliet Dusinberre: *Shakespeare and the Nature of Women*. London and Basingstoke: Macmillan, 1975.

Nigel Alexander: *Shakespeare: 'Measure for Measure'*. London: Arnold, 1975.

Rosalind Miles: *The Problem of 'Measure for Measure': A Historical Investigation*. London: Vision Press, 1976.

Ralph Berry: *On Directing Shakespeare: Interviews with Contemporary Directors*. London: Croom Helm, 1977. Enlarged edition: London: Hamish Hamilton, 1989.

Aspects of Shakespeare's 'Problem Plays', ed. Kenneth Muir and Stanley Wells. Cambridge: Cambridge University Press, 1982.

Political Shakespeare: New Essays in Cultural Materialism, ed. Jonathan Dollimore and Alan Sinfield. Manchester: Manchester University Press, 1985.

Cedric Watts: *William Shakespeare: 'Measure for Measure'*. Harmondsworth: Penguin, 1986.

Graham Nicholls: *'Measure for Measure': Text and Performance*. Basingstoke: Macmillan, 1986.

Harriett Hawkins: *Measure for Measure*. Brighton: Harvester, 1987.

T. F. Wharton: *'Measure for Measure'*. Basingstoke and London: Macmillan, 1989.

Longman Critical Essays: 'Measure for Measure', ed. Linda Cookson and Bryan Loughrey. Harlow: Longman, 1991.

Brian Vickers: *Appropriating Shakespeare: Contemporary Critical Quarrels*. New Haven and London: Yale University Press, 1993.

Kenneth S. Rothwell: *A History of Shakespeare on Screen: A Century of Film and Television*. Cambridge: Cambridge University Press, 1999.

John Sutherland and Cedric Watts: *Henry V, War Criminal? and Other Shakespeare Puzzles*. Oxford: Oxford University Press, 2000.

Nicholas Marsh: *Shakespeare: Three Problem Plays*. Basingstoke: Palgrave Macmillan, 2003.

Shakespeare: An Oxford Guide, ed. Stanley Wells and Lena Cowen Orlin. Oxford: Oxford University Press, 2003.

NOTE ON SHAKESPEARE

William Shakespeare was the son of a glover at Stratford-upon-Avon, and tradition gives his date of birth as 23 April, 1564; certainly, three days later, he was christened at the parish church. It is likely that he attended the local Grammar School but had no university education. Of his early career there is no record, though John Aubrey reports a claim that he was a rural schoolmaster. In 1582 Shakespeare married Anne Hathaway, with whom he had two daughters, Susanna and Judith, and a son, Hamnet, who died in 1596. How he became involved with the stage in London is uncertain, but by 1592 he was sufficiently established as a playwright to be criticised in print as a challengingly versatile 'upstart Crow'. He was a leading member of the Lord Chamberlain's company, which became the King's Men on the accession of James I in 1603. The players performed at a wide variety of locations: in the public theatre, at the royal court, in noblemen's houses, at colleges, and probably in the yards of inns. Being not only a playwright and an actor but also a 'sharer' (one of the owners of the company, entitled to a share of the profits), Shakespeare prospered greatly, as is proven by the numerous records of his financial transactions. Meanwhile, his sonnets expressed the poet's love for a beautiful young man and a 'dark lady'. Towards the end of his life, Shakespeare loosened his ties with London and retired to New Place, the large house in Stratford-upon-Avon which he had bought in 1597. He died on 23 April, 1616, and is buried in the location of his baptism, Holy Trinity Church. The earliest collected edition of his plays, the First Folio, was published in 1623, and its prefatory verse-tributes include Ben Jonson's famous declaration, 'He was not of an age, but for all time'.

ACKNOWLEDGEMENTS AND TEXTUAL MATTERS

I have consulted (and am indebted to) numerous editions of *Measure for Measure*, notably those by: Sir Arthur Quiller-Couch and John Dover Wilson (London: Cambridge University Press, 1922; rpt.,1950; revised and abridged as 'The Cambridge Pocket Shakespeare', ed. John Dover Wilson, 1958); James Winny (London: Hutchinson, 1959); Peter Alexander ('The Tudor Shakespeare': London and Glasgow: Collins, 1951; rpt., 1966); S. Nagarajan ('The Signet Classic Shakespeare': New York: New American Library, 1964); Ernst Leisi ('An Old-Spelling and Old-Meaning Edition': New York and London: Hafner, 1964); J. W. Lever ('The Arden Shakespeare': London: Methuen; Cambridge, Mass.: Harvard University Press; 1965); J. M. Nosworthy (the 'New Penguin Shakespeare': Harmondsworth: Penguin, 1969); G. Blakemore Evans *et al.* ('The Riverside Shakespeare'; Boston: Houghton Mifflin, 1974); Mark Eccles ('A New Variorum Edition': New York, Modern Language Association of America, 1980); N. W. Bawcutt ('The Oxford Shakespeare': Oxford: Oxford University Press, 1991; rpt., 1998); and Stephen Greenblatt *et al.* (*The Norton Shakespeare*: New York and London: Norton, 1997).

Measure for Measure was probably written in 1604, and the accounts of the Revels Office state that 'Mesur for Mesur' by 'Shaxberd' was performed in the banqueting hall at Whitehall (a royal palace) on 26 December, 1604. The earliest surviving text of the play is part of the First Folio, 1623; no previous quarto text is extant. A 'folio' is a book with relatively large pages, while a 'quarto' is a book with relatively small pages. More precisely, a folio volume is made of sheets of paper, each of which has been folded once to form two leaves and thus four pages, while each sheet of a quarto volume has been folded twice to form four leaves and thus eight pages. The First Folio (in latter times often designated 'F1') was the original 'collected edition' of Shakespeare's plays, published seven years after the playwright's death by two of the fellow-actors in his company, John Heminge (or Heminges) and Henry Condell. The fact that there is no early quarto text of *Measure for Measure* may seem to make the editor's task easier, by eliminating the problem of deciding between quite different readings. On the other hand, the editor's task is also harder, in the sense that there are no authoritative alternatives to consider if the copy-text seems faulty or obscure; and, in any case, posterity may thus lack some Shakespearian material that a quarto would have preserved. A Shakespearian play did not spring into existence fully-formed; it evolved.

Fortunately, the Folio text of *Measure for Measure* is, from the editorial viewpoint, of better quality than the average in that collection. Possibly an untidy script by Shakespeare was copied and partly tidied by a reasonably careful 'scrivener' or copyist. There remain, however, in addition to a sprinkling of small errors, various obscure passages which bear signs of textual corruption: notably 1.1.7-9, 3.1.95-8 and 3.2.254-7. These obscurities are discussed in my editorial notes. Furthermore, some editors speculate that Shakespeare's script was adapted by another writer before Folio publication. For example, in the 1988 'Compact Edition' of the Oxford University Press volume of Shakespeare's *Complete Works*, p. 789, we find this statement:

> Someone . . . seems to have supplied a new, seedy opening to Act 1, Scene 2; and an adapter seems also to have altered 3.1.517–4.1.63 [in this Wordsworth edition, 3.2.242–4.1.64,] by transposing the Duke's two soliloquies, by introducing a stanza from a popular song, and by supplying dialogue to follow it.

These claims have been disputed and are not generally accepted. There are no compelling grounds for regarding any of the material as non-Shakespearian: after all, Shakespeare is known to have revised his own scripts. Nevertheless, while retaining the F1 material, I have indicated in the notes such conjectures.

The present edition of *Measure for Measure* offers a practical compromise between the F1 version and modern requirements. In view of the usually good quality of the Folio text, I have followed its conventions somewhat more closely than have most editors. For instance, I have preserved (where they are logically and aurally satisfactory) many of its abundant colons and round brackets. I use a dash to indicate not only an interruption to a statement, or the start of a non-consecutive statement, but also a change of direction when a speaker turns from one addressee to another. The glossary explains archaisms and unfamiliar terms, while the annotations offer clarification of obscurities.

No edition of the play can claim to be definitive. This edition hopes to be useful.

MEASURE FOR MEASURE

CHARACTERS:

Vincentio, the DUKE *of Vienna.*

Lord ESCALUS.

Lord ANGELO.

MARIANA, *who loves Angelo.*

CLAUDIO, *a young gentleman.*

ISABELLA (ISABEL), *Claudio's sister.*

JULIETTA (JULIET), *Claudio's fiancée.*

LUCIO, *a gentleman.*

The PROVOST.

MISTRESS OVERDONE, *a brothel-keeper.*

POMPEY BUM, *servant to Overdone.*

ELBOW, *a constable.*

FROTH, *a gentleman.*

ABHORSON, *an executioner.*

BARNARDINE, *a prisoner.*

A JUSTICE.

FRIAR THOMAS; FRIAR PETER.

FRANCISCA, *a nun.*

VARRIUS, *a gentleman.*

Anonymous LORDS, GENTLEMEN, OFFICERS, SERVANTS, CITIZENS *and a* BOY.

The locations: various places in and near Vienna.

MEASURE FOR MEASURE[1]

ACT I, SCENE I.

Vienna. Inside the Duke's palace.

Enter the DUKE, ESCALUS *and* LORDS.

DUKE	Escalus!
ESCALUS	My lord?
DUKE	Of government the properties to unfold

Would seem in me t'affect speech and discourse,
Since I am put to know that your own science
Exceeds (in that) the lists of all advice
My strength can give you. Then no more remains
But that, to your sufficiency, as your worth is able,
And let them work.[2] The nature of our people,
Our city's institutions, and the terms   10
For common justice, y'are as pregnant in
As art and practice hath enrichèd any
That we remember. There is our commission,
From which we would not have you warp.
[*He hands it to Escalus. To a lord:*] Call hither,
I say, bid come before us, Angelo.   [*Exit a lord.*
[*To Escalus:*] What figure of us think you he will bear?
For you must know, we have with special soul
Elected him our absence to supply;
Lent him our terror, dressed him with our love,
And given his deputation all the organs   20
Of our own power. What think you of it?

ESCALUS   If any in Vienna be of worth
To undergo such ample grace and honour,
It is Lord Angelo.

Enter ANGELO.

DUKE   Look where he comes.

ANGELO   Always obedient to your Grace's will,
I come to know your pleasure.

DUKE   Angelo,

There is a kind of character in thy life
That to th'observer doth thy history
Fully unfold. Thyself and thy belongings
Are not thine own so proper as to waste   30
Thyself upon thy virtues, they on thee.
Heaven doth with us as we with torches do,
Not light them for themselves; for if our virtues
Did not go forth of us, 'twere all alike
As if we had them not. Spirits are not finely touched
But to fine issues;[3] nor Nature never lends
The smallest scruple of her excellence
But, like a thrifty goddess, she determines
Herself the glory of a creditor,
Both thanks and use.[4] But I do bend my speech   40
To one that can my part in him advértise.
Hold, therefore, Angelo:[5]
                              [*He offers a document to Angelo.*
In our remove be thou at full ourself;
Mortality and mercy in Vienna
Live in thy tongue and heart. Old Escalus,
Though first in question, is thy secondary.
Take thy commission.

ANGELO   Now, good my lord,
Let there be some more test made of my metal,
Before so noble and so great a figure
Be stamped upon it.

DUKE   No more evasion!   50
We have with a leavened and preparèd choice
Proceeded to you; therefore take your honours.
                              [*Angelo takes the document.*
Our haste from hence is of so quick condition
That it prefers itself, and leaves unquestioned
Matters of needful value. We shall write to you,
As time and our concernings shall impórtune,
How it goes with us, and do look to know
What doth befall you here. So, fare you well.
To th'hopeful execution do I leave you
Of your commissions.

ANGELO   Yet give leave, my lord,   60

	That we may bring you something on the way.
DUKE	My haste may not admit it;
	Nor need you (on mine honour) have to do
	With any scruple: your scope is as mine own,
	So to enforce or qualify the laws
	As to your soul seems good. Give me your hand;
	I'll privily away. I love the people,
	But do not like to stage me to their eyes;
	Though it do well, I do not relish well
	Their loud applause and *Ave*s vehement;[6]
	Nor do I think the man of safe discretion
	That does affect it. Once more, fare you well.
ANGELO	The heavens give safety to your purposes, —
ESCALUS	Lead forth and bring you back in happiness!
DUKE	I thank you. Fare you well. [*Exit Duke.*
ESCALUS	I shall desire you, sir, to give me leave
	To have free speech with you; and it concerns me
	To look into the bottom of my place:
	A pow'r I have, but of what strength and nature
	I am not yet instructed.
ANGELO	'Tis so with me. Let us withdraw together,
	And we may soon our satisfaction have,
	Touching that point.
ESCALUS	I'll wait upon your Honour.
	[*Exeunt.*

Line numbers: 70 (at "Their loud applause…"), 80 (at "I am not yet instructed.")

SCENE 2.

A street.

Enter LUCIO *and two other* GENTLEMEN.

LUCIO   If the Duke, with the other dukes, come not to composition with the King of Hungary, why then all the
dukes fall upon the King.

GENT. I   Heaven grant us its peace, but not the King of Hungary's!

GENT. 2   Amen.

LUCIO   Thou conclud'st like the sanctimonious pirate that went
to sea with the Ten Commandments, but scraped one
out of the table.[7]

GENT. 2   'Thou shalt not steal'?

LUCIO   Ay, that he razed.   10

GENT. I   Why, 'twas a commandment to command the captain
and all the rest from their functions: they put forth to
steal. There's not a soldier of us all that, in the thanks-
giving before meat, do relish the petition well that
prays for peace.

GENT. 2   I never heard any soldier dislike it.

LUCIO   I believe thee; for I think thou never wast where grace
was said.

GENT. 2   No? A dozen times at least.

GENT. I   What? In metre?   20

LUCIO   In any proportion or in any language.

GENT. I   I think, or in any religion.

LUCIO   Ay, why not? Grace is grace, despite of all controversy;
as, for example, thou thyself art a wicked villain, despite
of all grace.

GENT. I   Well, there went but a pair of shears between us.

LUCIO   I grant; as there may between the lists and the velvet.
Thou art the list.

GENT. I   And thou the velvet. Thou art good velvet: thou'rt a
three-piled piece, I warrant thee. I had as lief be a list   30
of an English kersey as be piled, as thou art piled, for a
French velvet. Do I speak feelingly now?[8]

LUCIO   I think thou dost; and, indeed, with most painful feeling
            of thy speech. I will, out of thine own confession,
            learn to begin thy health; but, whilst I live, forget to
            drink after thee.

GENT. I   I think I have done myself wrong, have I not?

GENT. 2   Yes, that thou hast, whether thou art tainted or free.

                Enter MISTRESS OVERDONE.

LUCIO   Behold, behold, where Madam Mitigation comes! I
            have purchased as many diseases under her roof as come   40
            to —

GENT. 2   To what, I pray?

GENT. I   Judge.

GENT. 2   To three thousand dolours a year.

GENT. I   Ay, and more.

LUCIO   A French crown more.

GENT. I   Thou art always figuring diseases in me, but thou art
            full of error: I am sound.

LUCIO   Nay, not (as one would say) healthy; but so sound as
            things that are hollow: thy bones are hollow; impiety   50
            has made a feast of thee.

GENT. I   [*to Overdone:*] How now? Which of your hips has the
            most profound sciatica?

OVERDONE Well, well! There's one yonder, arrested and carried to
            prison, was worth five thousand of you all.

GENT. I   Who's that, I pray thee?

OVERDONE Marry, sir, that's Claudio, Signor Claudio.

GENT. I   Claudio to prison? 'Tis not so.

OVERDONE Nay, but I know 'tis so: I saw him arrested; saw him
            carried away; and, which is more, within these three   60
            days his head to be chopped off.

LUCIO   But, after all this fooling, I would not have it so. Art
            thou sure of this?

OVERDONE I am too sure of it; and it is for getting Madam Julietta
            with child.

LUCIO   [*to gentlemen:*] Believe me, this may be. He promised
            to meet me two hours since, and he was ever precise
            in promise-keeping.

GENT. 2   Besides, you know, it draws something near to the
            speech we had to such a purpose.   70

GENT. 1   But most of all agreeing with the proclamation.

LUCIO   Away: let's go learn the truth of it.

                              [*Exeunt Lucio and gentlemen.*

OVERDONE Thus, what with the war, what with the sweat, what
          with the gallows, and what with poverty, I am custom-
          shrunk.[9]

                       Enter POMPEY.

          How now? What's the news with you?

POMPEY   Yonder man is carried to prison.

OVERDONE Well, what has he done?

POMPEY   A woman.

OVERDONE But what's his offence?   80

POMPEY   Groping for trouts in a peculiar river.

OVERDONE What? Is there a maid with child by him?

POMPEY   No; but there's a woman with maid by him.[10] You
          have not heard of the proclamation, have you?

OVERDONE What proclamation, man?

POMPEY   All houses in the suburbs of Vienna must be plucked
          down.

OVERDONE And what shall become of those in the city?

POMPEY   They shall stand for seed; they had gone down too, but
          that a wise burgher put in for them.   90

OVERDONE But shall all our houses of resort in the suburbs be
          pulled down?

POMPEY   To the ground, mistress.

OVERDONE Why, here's a change indeed in the commonwealth!
          What shall become of me?

POMPEY   Come, fear not you: good counsellors lack no clients.
          Though you change your place, you need not change
          your trade; I'll be your tapster still. Courage, there will
          be pity taken on you: you that have worn your eyes
          almost out in the service, you will be considered.   100

OVERDONE [*seeing people approaching:*] What's to do here, Thomas
          Tapster? Let's withdraw.

POMPEY   Here comes Signor Claudio, led by the Provost to
          prison; and there's Madam Juliet.   [*Exeunt.*

     Enter the PROVOST, CLAUDIO, JULIET *and* OFFICERS; *followed by*
                 LUCIO *and the two* GENTLEMEN.

CLAUDIO	Fellow, why dost thou show me thus to th'world?
	Bear me to prison, where I am committed.
PROVOST	I do it not in evil disposition,
	But from Lord Angelo by special charge.
CLAUDIO	Thus can the demi-god, Authority,
	Make us pay down for our offence by weight. 110
	The words of Heaven: on whom it will, it will;
	On whom it will not, so; yet still 'tis just.[11]
LUCIO	Why, how now, Claudio? Whence comes this restraint?
CLAUDIO	From too much liberty, my Lucio, liberty.
	As surfeit is the father of much fast,
	So every scope by the immoderate use
	Turns to restraint. Our natures do pursue,
	Like rats that ravin down their proper bane,
	A thirsty evil; and when we drink, we die.
LUCIO	If I could speak so wisely under an arrest, I would send 120
	for certain of my creditors; and yet, to say the truth, I
	had as lief have the foppery of freedom as the morality
	of imprisonment. What's thy offence, Claudio?
CLAUDIO	What but to speak of would offend again.
LUCIO	What, is't murder?
CLAUDIO	No.
LUCIO	Lechery?
CLAUDIO	Call it so.
PROVOST	Away, sir; you must go.
CLAUDIO	One word, good friend. – Lucio, a word with you. 130
LUCIO	A hundred, if they'll do you any good.
	Is lechery so looked after?
CLAUDIO	Thus stands it with me: upon a true contráct
	I got possession of Julietta's bed.
	You know the lady; she is fast my wife,
	Save that we do the denunciation lack
	Of outward order. This we came not to,
	Only for propagation of a dower
	Remaining in the coffer of her friends,
	From whom we thought it meet to hide our love 140
	Till time had made them for us. But, it chances,
	The stealth of our most mutual entertainment,
	With character too gross, is writ on Juliet.

LUCIO   With child, perhaps?

CLAUDIO   Unhappily, even so.
            And the new deputy now for the Duke:
            Whether it be the fault and glimpse of newness,
            Or whether that the body public be
            A horse whereon the governor doth ride,
            Who, newly in the seat, that it may know
            He can command, lets it straight feel the spur;   150
            Whether the tyranny be in his place,
            Or in his eminence that fills it up,
            I stagger in: but this new governor
            Awakes me all the enrollèd penalties
            Which have (like unscoured armour) hung by th'wall
            So long that nineteen zodiacs[12] have gone round,
            And none of them been worn; and, for a name,
            Now puts the drowsy and neglected act
            Freshly on me: 'tis surely for a name.

LUCIO   I warrant it is; and thy head stands so tickle on thy   160
            shoulders that a milkmaid, if she be in love, may sigh it
            off. Send after the Duke, and appeal to him.

CLAUDIO   I have done so, but he's not to be found.
            I prithee, Lucio, do me this kind service:
            This day my sister should the cloister enter,
            And there receive her approbation;
            Acquaint her with the danger of my state;
            Implore her, in my voice, that she make friends
            To the strict deputy; bid herself assay him:
            I have great hope in that; for in her youth   170
            There is a prone and speechless dialect,
            Such as move men; beside, she hath prosperous art
            When she will play with reason and discourse,
            And well she can persuade.

LUCIO   I pray she may; as well for the encouragement of the like,
            which else would stand under grievous imposition, as for
            the enjoying of thy life, who I would be sorry should be
            thus foolishly lost at a game of tick-tack. I'll to her.

CLAUDIO   I thank you, good friend Lucio.

LUCIO   Within two hours.   180

CLAUDIO   Come, officer, away.   [Exeunt.

SCENE 3.

A monastery.

Enter the DUKE *and* FRIAR THOMAS.

DUKE   No, holy father; throw away that thought;
Believe not that the dribbling dart of love
Can pierce a cómplete bosom. Why I desire thee
To give me secret harbour hath a purpose
More grave and wrinkled than the aims and ends
Of burning youth.

FRIAR   May your Grace speak of it?

DUKE   My holy sir, none better knows than you
How I have ever loved the life removed,
And held in idle price to haunt assemblies
Where youth, and cost, a witless bravery keeps.[13]   10
I have delivered to Lord Angelo
(A man of stricture and firm abstinence)
My absolute power and place here in Vienna,
And he supposes me travailed to Poland;
For so I have strewed it in the common ear,
And so it is received. Now, pious sir,
You will demand of me why I do this.

FRIAR   Gladly, my lord.

DUKE   We have strict statutes and most biting laws
(The needful bits and curbs to headstrong steeds),   20
Which for this fourteen years we have let sleep,[14]
Even like an o'ergrown lion in a cave,
That goes not out to prey. Now, as fond fathers,
Having bound up the threat'ning twigs of birch,
Only to stick it in their children's sight
For terror, not to use: in time the rod
Becomes more mocked than feared; so our decrees,[15]
Dead to infliction, to themselves are dead;
And Liberty plucks Justice by the nose,
The baby beats the nurse, and quite athwart   30

Goes all decorum.

FRIAR   It rested in your Grace
To unloose this tied-up justice when you pleased;
And it in you more dreadful would have seemed
Than in Lord Angelo.

DUKE   I do fear, too dreadful.
Sith 'twas my fault to give the people scope,
'Twould be my tyranny to strike and gall them
For what I bid them do; for we bid this be done,
When evil deeds have their permissive pass
And not the punishment. Therefore, indeed, my father,
I have on Angelo imposed the office,   40
Who may, in th'ambush of my name, strike home,
And yet my nature never in the fight
To do in slander.[16] And, to behold his sway,
I will, as 'twere a brother of your Order,
Visit both prince and people. Therefore, I prithee,
Supply me with the habit, and instruct me
How I may formally in person bear me
Like a true friar. Moe reasons for this action
At our more leisure shall I render you.
Only, this one: Lord Angelo is precise;   50
Stands at a guard with envy; scarce confesses
That his blood flows, or that his appetite
Is more to bread than stone. Hence shall we see,
If power change purpose, what our seemers be.
                                        [Exeunt.

SCENE 4.

Inside a nunnery, near its locked entrance.

Enter ISABELLA *and* FRANCISCA.

ISABELLA   And have you nuns no farther privileges?
FRANCISCA Are not these large enough?
ISABELLA   Yes, truly; I speak not as desiring more,
    But rather wishing a more strict restraint
    Upon the Sisterhood, the votarists of Saint Clare.[17]
LUCIO   [*beyond:*] Ho! Peace be in this place!
ISABELLA   [*to Francisca:*]   Who's that which calls?
FRANCISCA It is a man's voice. Gentle Isabella,
    Turn you the key, and know his business of him:
    You may, I may not; you are yet unsworn.
    When you have vowed, you must not speak with men   10
    But in the presence of the prioress;
    Then, if you speak, you must not show your face,
    Or, if you show your face, you must not speak.
              [*Lucio calls.*
    He calls again: I pray you answer him. [*Exit Francisca.*
ISABELLA   Peace and prosperity! Who is't that calls?
            [*She unlocks the door.*

Enter LUCIO.

LUCIO   Hail, virgin (if you be), as those cheek–roses
    Proclaim you are no less. Can you so stead me
    As bring me to the sight of Isabella,
    A novice of this place, and the fair sister
    To her unhappy brother Claudio?   20
ISABELLA   'Why her "unhappy brother"?', let me ask;
    The rather, for I now must make you know
    I am that Isabella, and his sister.
LUCIO   Gentle and fair, your brother kindly greets you.
    Not to be weary with you, he's in prison.
ISABELLA   Woe me! For what?
LUCIO   For that which, if myself might be his judge,

	He should receive his punishment in thanks:	
	He hath got his friend with child.	
ISABELLA	Sir, make me not your story.	
LUCIO	It is true.	30

    I would not (though 'tis my familiar sin
    With maids to seem the lapwing,[18] and to jest,
    Tongue far from heart) play with all virgins so:
    I hold you as a thing enskied and sainted
    By your renouncement, an immortal spirit,
    And to be talked with in sincerity,
    As with a saint.

ISABELLA You do blaspheme the good, in mocking me.

LUCIO Do not believe it. Fewness and truth, 'tis thus:
    Your brother and his lover have embraced: 40
    As those that feed grow full, as blossoming time
    That from the seedness the bare fallow brings
    To teeming foison, even so her plenteous womb
    Expresseth his full tilth and husbandry.

ISABELLA Some one with child by him? My cousin Juliet?

LUCIO Is she your cousin?

ISABELLA Adoptedly, as school-maids change their names
    By vain though apt affection.

LUCIO   She it is.

ISABELLA O, let him marry her!

LUCIO   This is the point.
    The Duke is very strangely gone from hence;   50
    Bore many gentlemen (myself being one)
    In hand, and hope of action; but we do learn,
    By those that know the very nerves of state,
    His givings-out were of an infinite distance
    From his true-meant design. Upon his place
    (And with full line of his authority)
    Governs Lord Angelo, a man whose blood
    Is very snow-broth, one who never feels
    The wanton stings and motions of the sense,
    But doth rebate and blunt his natural edge   60
    With profits of the mind, study and fast.
    He (to give fear to use and liberty,
    Which have for long run by the hideous law,

As mice by lions,) hath picked out an act
Under whose heavy sense your brother's life
Falls into forfeit; he arrests him on it,
And follows close the rigour of the statute,
To make him an example. All hope is gone,
Unless you have the grace by your fair prayer
To soften Angelo. And that's my pith of business   70
'Twixt you and your poor brother.

ISABELLA   Doth he so seek his life?

LUCIO   Has censured him
Already, and, as I hear, the Provost hath
A warrant for his execution.

ISABELLA   Alas! What poor ability's in me
To do him good?

LUCIO   Assay the pow'r you have.

ISABELLA   My power? Alas, I doubt.

LUCIO   Our doubts are traitors,
And make us lose the good we oft might win,
By fearing to attempt. Go to Lord Angelo,
And let him learn to know, when maidens sue,   80
Men give like gods; but when they weep and kneel,
All their petitions are as freely theirs
As they themselves would owe them.

ISABELLA   I'll see what I can do.

LUCIO   But speedily.

ISABELLA   I will about it straight;
No longer staying but to give the Mother
Notice of my affair. I humbly thank you.
Commend me to my brother; soon at night
I'll send him certain word of my success.

LUCIO   I take my leave of you.

ISABELLA   Good sir, adieu.   [*Exeunt.*   90

ACT 2, SCENE 1.

Inside a court of justice.

Enter ANGELO, ESCALUS, *a* JUSTICE *and* SERVANTS.

ANGELO   We must not make a scarecrow of the law,
Setting it up to fear the birds of prey,
And let it keep one shape till custom make it
Their perch and not their terror.

ESCALUS   Ay, but yet
Let us be keen, and rather cut a little
Than fall and bruise to death. Alas, this gentleman,
Whom I would save, had a most noble father.
Let but your Honour know
(Whom I believe to be most strait in virtue)
That, in the working of your own affections,   10
Had time cohered with place, or place with wishing,
Or that the resolute acting of our blood[19]
Could have attained th'effect of your own purpose,
Whether you had not sometime in your life
Erred in this point, which now you censure him,
And pulled the law upon you.

ANGELO   'Tis one thing to be tempted, Escalus;
Another thing to fall. I not deny
The jury, passing on the prisoner's life,
May in the sworn twelve have a thief or two   20
Guiltier than him they try. What's open made to justice,
That justice seizes. What knows the laws
That thieves do pass on thieves?[20] 'Tis very pregnant,
The jewel that we find, we stoop and take't,
Because we see it; but what we do not see,
We tread upon, and never think of it.
You may not so extenuate his offence
For I have had such faults; but rather tell me,
When I, that censure him, do so offend,
Let mine own judgement pattern out my death,   30
And nothing come in partial.[21] Sir, he must die.

Enter the PROVOST.

ESCALUS   Be it as your wisdom will.

ANGELO   Where is the Provost?

PROVOST   Here, if it like your Honour.

ANGELO   . See that Claudio
          Be executed by nine tomorrow morning;
          Bring him his cónfessor; let him be prepared;
          For that's the utmost of his pilgrimage.   [*Exit Provost.*

ESCALUS   [*aside:*] Well, Heaven forgive him, and forgive us all!
          'Some rise by sin, and some by virtue fall':
          Some run from brakes of vice, and answer none,
          And some condemnèd for a fault alone.[22]   40

          Enter ELBOW *and* OFFICERS *with* FROTH *and* POMPEY.

ELBOW   Come, bring them away: if these be good people in a
          commonweal, that do nothing but use their abuses in
          common houses, I know no law: bring them away.

ANGELO   How now, sir? What's your name? And what's the
          matter?

ELBOW   If it please your Honour, I am the poor Duke's constable,
          and my name is Elbow; I do lean upon justice, sir, and
          do bring in here, before your good Honour, two notor-
          ious benefactors.[23]

ANGELO   'Benefactors'? Well, what 'benefactors' are they? Are   50
          they not malefactors?

ELBOW   If it please your Honour, I know not well what they are;
          but precise villains they are, that I am sure of, and void
          of all profanation in the world that good Christians
          ought to have.

ESCALUS   [*to Angelo:*] This comes off well; here's a wise officer.

ANGELO   [*to Elbow:*] Go to; what quality are they of? 'Elbow' is
          your name? Why dost thou not speak, Elbow?

POMPEY   He cannot, sir; he's out at elbow.

ANGELO   What are you, sir?   60

ELBOW   He, sir? A tapster, sir; parcel bawd; one that serves a
          bad woman, whose house, sir, was, as they say,
          plucked down in the suburbs; and now she professes a
          hot-house, which, I think, is a very ill house too.

ESCALUS   How know you that?

ELBOW	My wife, sir, whom I detest before Heaven and your Honour –
ESCALUS	How? Thy wife?
ELBOW	Ay, sir; whom, I thank Heaven, is an honest woman –
ESCALUS	Dost thou detest her therefore?

70

ELBOW	I say, sir, I will detest myself also, as well as she, that this house, if it be not a bawd's house, it is pity of her life, for it is a naughty house.
ESCALUS	How dost thou know that, constable?
ELBOW	Marry, sir, by my wife; who, if she had been a woman cardinally given, might have been accused in fornication, adultery, and all uncleanliness there.
ESCALUS	By the woman's means?
ELBOW	Ay, sir, by Mistress Overdone's means; but as she spit in his face, so she defied him.

80

POMPEY	Sir, if it please your Honour, this is not so.
ELBOW	Prove it before these varlets here, thou honourable man, prove it.
ESCALUS	[to Angelo:] Do you hear how he misplaces?
POMPEY	Sir, she came in great with child, and longing (saving your Honour's reverence) for stewed prunes.[24] Sir, we had but two in the house, which at that very distant time stood, as it were, in a fruit-dish, a dish of some three pence; your Honours have seen such dishes: they are not China dishes, but very good dishes.

90

ESCALUS	Go to, go to; no matter for the dish, sir.
POMPEY	No, indeed, sir, not of a pin; you are therein in the right; but to the point. As I say, this Mistress Elbow, being (as I say) with child, and being great-bellied, and longing (as I said) for prunes; and having but two in the dish (as I said), Master Froth here, this very man, having eaten the rest (as I said), and (as I say) paying for them very honestly – for, as you know, Master Froth, I could not give you three pence again –
FROTH	No, indeed.

100

POMPEY	Very well; you being then (if you be remembered) cracking the stones of the foresaid prunes –
FROTH	Ay, so I did indeed.
POMPEY	Why, very well; I telling you then (if you be remembered),

that such a one, and such a one, were past cure of the
thing you wot of, unless they kept very good diet, as I
told you –

FROTH   All this is true.

POMPEY   Why, very well then –

ESCALUS   Come; you are a tedious fool: to the purpose: what was   110
done to Elbow's wife that he hath cause to complain of?
Come me to what was done to her.

POMPEY   Sir, your Honour cannot come to that yet.

ESCALUS   No sir, nor I mean it not.[25]

POMPEY   Sir, but you shall come to it, by your Honour's leave.
And I beseech you, look into Master Froth here, sir, a
man of fourscore pound a year; whose father died at
Hallowmas – was't not at Hallowmas, Master Froth?

FROTH   All-hallond Eve.

POMPEY   Why, very well; I hope here be truths. He, sir, sitting   120
(as I say) in a lower chair, sir; 'twas in the Bunch of
Grapes – where, indeed, you have a delight to sit, have
you not?

FROTH   I have so; because it is an open room, and good for
winter.

POMPEY   Why, very well then; I hope here be truths.

ANGELO   [to Escalus:] This will last out a night in Russia,
When nights are longest there. I'll take my leave,
And leave you to the hearing of the cause,
Hoping you'll find good cause to whip them all.   130

ESCALUS   I think no less. Good morrow to your lordship.

                                              [Exit Angelo.

[To Pompey:] Now, sir, come on; what was done to
Elbow's wife, once more?

POMPEY   'Once', sir? There was nothing done to her once.

ELBOW   I beseech you, sir, ask him what this man did to my
wife.

POMPEY   I beseech your Honour, ask me.

ESCALUS   Well, sir, what did this gentleman to her?

POMPEY   I beseech you, sir, look in this gentleman's face. – Good
Master Froth, look upon his Honour; 'tis for a good   140
purpose. – Doth your Honour mark his face?

ESCALUS   Ay sir, very well.

POMPEY	Nay, I beseech you, mark it well.
ESCALUS	Well, I do so.
POMPEY	Doth your Honour see any harm in his face?
ESCALUS	Why, no.
POMPEY	I'll be supposed upon a book, his face is the worst thing about him. Good then: if his face be the worst thing about him, how could Master Froth do the constable's wife any harm? I would know that of your Honour. 150
ESCALUS	He's in the right, constable; what say you to it?
ELBOW	First, and it like you, the house is a respected house; next, this is a respected fellow; and his mistress is a respected woman.
POMPEY	[to Escalus:] By this hand, sir, his wife is a more respected person than any of us all.
ELBOW	Varlet, thou liest; thou liest, wicked varlet: the time is yet to come that she was ever respected with man, woman, or child.
POMPEY	Sir, she was respected with him before he married 160 with her.
ESCALUS	Which is the wiser here, Justice or Iniquity? Is this true?
ELBOW	O thou caitiff! O thou varlet! O thou wicked Hannibal![26] I respected with her before I was married to her? – If ever I was respected with her, or she with me, let not your Worship think me the poor Duke's officer. – Prove this, thou wicked Hannibal, or I'll have mine action of battery on thee.
ESCALUS	If he took you a box o'th'ear, you might have your action of slander too. 170
ELBOW	Marry, I thank your good Worship for it. What is't your Worship's pleasure I shall do with this wicked caitiff?
ESCALUS	Truly, officer, because he hath some offences in him that thou wouldst discover if thou couldst, let him continue in his courses till thou know'st what they are.
ELBOW	Marry, I thank your Worship for it. – Thou seest, thou wicked varlet, now, what's come upon thee. Thou art to continue now, thou varlet; thou art to continue.
ESCALUS	[to Froth:] Where were you born, friend?
FROTH	Here in Vienna, sir. 180
ESCALUS	Are you of fourscore pounds a year?

FROTH	Yes, and't please you, sir.
ESCALUS	So. [*To Pompey:*] What trade are you of, sir?
POMPEY	A tapster, a poor widow's tapster.
ESCALUS	Your mistress' name?
POMPEY	Mistress Overdone.
ESCALUS	Hath she had any more than one husband?
POMPEY	Nine, sir. Overdone by the last.[27]

ESCALUS   Nine! – Come hither to me, Master Froth. Master
            Froth, I would not have you acquainted with tapsters: 190
            they will draw you, Master Froth, and you will hang
            them.[28] Get you gone, and let me hear no more of you.

FROTH   I thank your Worship. For mine own part, I never
            come into any room in a tap-house but I am drawn in.

ESCALUS   Well, no more of it, Master Froth; farewell. [*Exit Froth.*
            Come you hither to me, Master Tapster. What's your
            name, Master Tapster?

POMPEY   Pompey.

ESCALUS   What else?

POMPEY   Bum, sir.   200

ESCALUS   Troth, and your bum is the greatest thing about you;
            so that, in the beastliest sense, you are Pompey the
            Great. Pompey, you are partly a bawd, Pompey, how-
            soever you colour it in being a tapster; are you not?
            Come, tell me true; it shall be the better for you.

POMPEY   Truly, sir, I am a poor fellow that would live.

ESCALUS   How would you live, Pompey? By being a bawd? What
            do you think of the trade, Pompey? Is it a lawful trade?

POMPEY   If the law would allow it, sir.

ESCALUS   But the law will *not* allow it, Pompey; nor it shall not   210
            be allowed in Vienna.

POMPEY   Does your Worship mean to geld and splay all the
            youth of the city?

ESCALUS   No, Pompey.

POMPEY   Truly, sir, in my poor opinion, they will to't then. If
            your Worship will take order for the drabs and the
            knaves, you need not to fear the bawds.

ESCALUS   There is pretty orders beginning, I can tell you: it is
            but heading and hanging.

POMPEY   If you head and hang all that offend that way but for ten   220

year together, you'll be glad to give out a commission
for more heads. If this law hold in Vienna ten year, I'll
rent the fairest house in it, after threepence a bay. If you
live to see this come to pass, say Pompey told you so.

ESCALUS   Thank you, good Pompey; and, in requital of your
prophecy, hark you: I advise you, let me not find you
before me again upon any complaint whatsoever – no,
not for dwelling where you do; if I do, Pompey, I shall
beat you to your tent, and prove a shrewd Cæsar to
you:[29] in plain dealing, Pompey, I shall have you   230
whipped. So for this time, Pompey, fare you well.

POMPEY   I thank your Worship for your good counsel; [*aside:*]
but I shall follow it as the flesh and fortune shall better
determine.
            Whip me? No, no; let carman whip his jade;
            The valiant heart's not whipped out of his trade. [*Exit.*

ESCALUS   Come hither to me, Master Elbow; come hither, Master
Constable. How long have you been in this place of
constable?

ELBOW   Seven year and a half, sir.   240

ESCALUS   I thought, by the readiness in the office, you had con-
tinued in it some time. You say seven years together?

ELBOW   And a half, sir.

ESCALUS   Alas, it hath been great pains to you: they do you
wrong to put you so oft upon't. Are there not men in
your ward sufficient to serve it?

ELBOW   Faith, sir, few of any wit in such matters; as they are
chosen, they are glad to choose me for them; I do it
for some piece of money, and go through with all.

ESCALUS   Look you, bring me in the names of some six or seven,   250
the most sufficient of your parish.

ELBOW   To your Worship's house, sir?

ESCALUS   To my house. Fare you well.   [*Exit Elbow.*
            [*To Justice:*] What's o'clock, think you?

JUSTICE   Eleven, sir.

ESCALUS   I pray you home to dinner with me.

JUSTICE   I humbly thank you.

ESCALUS   It grieves me for the death of Claudio;
            But there's no remedy.

JUSTICE	Lord Angelo is severe.
ESCALUS	It is but needful: 260

Mercy is not itself that oft looks so;
Pardon is still the nurse of second woe.
But yet, poor Claudio! There is no remedy.
Come, sir.   [*Exeunt.*

SCENE 2.

A room in the court of justice.

Enter the PROVOST *and a* SERVANT.

SERVANT	He's hearing of a cause; he will come straight.

SERVANT He's hearing of a cause; he will come straight.
I'll tell him of you.
PROVOST   Pray you, do. [*Exit servant.*]
                                    I'll know
His pleasure; may be he will relent. Alas,
He hath but as offended in a dream.
All sects, all ages, smack of this vice; and he
To die for't?

Enter ANGELO.

ANGELO Now, what's the matter, Provost?
PROVOST Is it your will Claudio shall die tomorrow?
ANGELO Did not I tell thee yea? Hadst thou not order?
Why dost thou ask again?   10
PROVOST Lest I might be too rash:[30]
Under your good correction, I have seen
When, after execution, judgement hath
Repented o'er his doom.
ANGELO Go to; let that be mine.
Do you your office, or give up your place,
And you shall well be spared.
PROVOST I crave your Honour's pardon.
What shall be done, sir, with the groaning Juliet?
She's very near her hour.
ANGELO   Dispose of her   20
To some more fitter place, and that with speed.

Enter SERVANT.

SERVANT Here is the sister of the man condemned
Desires accéss to you.
ANGELO   Hath he a sister?
PROVOST Ay, my good lord; a very virtuous maid,
And to be shortly of a sisterhood,

	If not already.
ANGELO	Well, let her be admitted. [*Exit servant.*
	See you the fornicatress be removed.
	Let her have needful but not lavish means:
	There shall be order for't.

Enter LUCIO *and* ISABELLA.

PROVOST   [*going:*] 'Save your Honour![31]   30

ANGELO   Stay a little while. [*To Isabella:*] Y'are welcome; what's
                                             your will?

ISABELLA   I am a woeful suitor to your Honour,
           Please but your Honour hear me.

ANGELO   Well, what's your suit?

ISABELLA   There is a vice that most I do abhor,
           And most desire should meet the blow of justice;
           For which I would not plead, but that I must;
           For which I must not plead, but that I am
           At war 'twixt will and will not.

ANGELO   Well: the matter?

ISABELLA   I have a brother is condemned to die;
           I do beseech you, let it be his fault,   40
           And not my brother.

PROVOST   [*aside:*]   Heaven give thee moving graces.

ANGELO   Condemn the fault, and not the actor of it?
           Why, every fault's condemn'd ere it be done.
           Mine were the very cipher of a function,
           To fine the faults whose fine stands in recórd,
           And let go by the actor.

ISABELLA   O just but severe law!
           I had a brother, then. Heaven keep your Honour!

LUCIO   [*aside to Isabella:*] Give't not o'er so; to him again,
                                         entreat him,
           Kneel down before him, hang upon his gown;   50
           You are too cold: if you should need a pin,
           You could not with more tame a tongue desire it:
           To him, I say.

ISABELLA   [*to Angelo:*] Must he needs die?

ANGELO   Maiden, no remedy.

ISABELLA   Yes; I do think that you might pardon him,

	And neither Heaven nor man grieve at the mercy.
ANGELO	I will not do't.
ISABELLA	But can you, if you would?
ANGELO	Look, what I will not, that I cannot do.
ISABELLA	But might you do't, and do the world no wrong,

And neither Heaven nor man grieve at the mercy.

ANGELO I will not do't.

ISABELLA   But can you, if you would?

ANGELO Look, what I will not, that I cannot do.

ISABELLA But might you do't, and do the world no wrong,
If so your heart were touched with that remorse   60
As mine is to him?

ANGELO   He's sentenced; 'tis too late.

LUCIO [*aside to Isabella:*] You are too cold.

ISABELLA 'Too late'? Why no: I, that do speak a word,
May call it back again. Well, believe this:[32]
No ceremony that to great ones longs,
Not the king's crown nor the deputed sword,
The marshal's truncheon nor the judge's robe,
Become them with one half so good a grace
As mercy does.
If he had been as you, and you as he,   70
You would have slipped like him; but he like you
Would not have been so stern.[33]

ANGELO   Pray you be gone.

ISABELLA I would to Heaven I had your potency,
And you were Isabel! Should it then be thus?
No; I would tell what 'twere to be a judge,
And what a prisoner.

LUCIO [*aside to Isabella:*]   Ay, touch him; there's the vein.

ANGELO Your brother is a forfeit of the law,
And you but waste your words.

ISABELLA   Alas, alas!
Why, all the souls that were, were forfeit once;
And He that might the vantage best have took   80
Found out the remedy. How would you be
If He, which is the top of judgement, should
But judge you as you are? O, think on that,
And mercy then will breathe within your lips,
Like man new-made.[34]

ANGELO   Be you content, fair maid;
It is the law, not I, condemn your brother.
Were he my kinsman, brother, or my son,
It should be thus with him: he must die tomorrow.

ISABELLA   Tomorrow? O, that's sudden; spare him, spare him!
           He's not prepared for death. Even for our kitchens   90
           We kill the fowl of season: shall we serve Heaven
           With less respect than we do minister
           To our gross selves? Good, good my lord, bethink you:
           Who is it that hath died for this offence?
           There's many have committed it.
LUCIO   [aside to her:]   Ay, well said.
ANGELO   The law hath not been dead, though it hath slept.
           Those many had not dared to do that evil
           If the first that did th'edict infringe
           Had answered for his deed. Now 'tis awake,
           Takes note of what is done, and, like a prophet,   100
           Looks in a glass that shows what future evils,
           Either new or, by remissness, new-conceived,
           And so in progress to be hatch'd and born,
           Are now to have no successive degrees,
           But ere they live to end.[35]
ISABELLA   Yet show some pity.
ANGELO   I show it most of all when I show justice;
           For then I pity those I do not know,
           Which a dismissed offence would after gall,
           And do him right that, answering one foul wrong,
           Lives not to act another. Be satisfied;   110
           Your brother dies tomorrow; be content.
ISABELLA   So you must be the first that gives this sentence,
           And he that suffers. O, it is excellent
           To have a giant's strength, but it is tyrannous
           To use it like a giant.
LUCIO   [aside to her:]   That's well said.
ISABELLA   Could great men thunder
           As Jove himself does, Jove would never be quiet,
           For every pelting petty officer
           Would use his Heaven for thunder, nothing but
                                              thunder!
           Merciful Heaven,   120
           Thou rather, with thy sharp and sulphurous bolt,
           Splits the unwedgeable and gnarlèd oak
           Than the soft myrtle.[36] But man, proud man,

Dressed in a little brief authority,
Most ignorant of what he's most assured
(His glassy essence), like an angry ape
Plays such fantastic tricks before high Heaven
As makes the angels weep; who, with our spleens,
Would all themselves laugh mortal.[37]

LUCIO   [*aside to her:*] O, to him, to him, wench: he will relent; 130
           He's coming; I perceive't.

PROVOST   [*aside:*]   Pray Heaven she win him!

ISABELLA   We cannot weigh our brother with ourself.[38]
           Great men may jest with saints: 'tis wit in them;
           But in the less, foul profanation.

LUCIO   [*aside to her:*] Thou'rt i'th'right, girl; more o'that.

ISABELLA   That in the captain's but a choleric word,
           Which in the soldier is flat blasphemy.

LUCIO   [*aside to her:*] Art avised o'that? More on't.

ANGELO   Why do you put these sayings upon me?

ISABELLA   Because authority, though it err like others,   140
           Hath yet a kind of medicine in itself
           That skins the vice o'th'top. Go to your bosom,
           Knock there, and ask your heart what it doth know
           That's like my brother's fault: if it confess
           A natural guiltiness, such as is his,
           Let it not sound a thought upon your tongue
           Against my brother's life.

ANGELO   [*aside, turning away:*]   She speaks, and 'tis
           Such sense that my sense breeds with it. – Fare you well.

ISABELLA   Gentle my lord, turn back.

ANGELO   I will bethink me. Come again tomorrow.   150

ISABELLA   Hark how I'll bribe you; good my lord, turn back.

ANGELO   How? 'Bribe' me?[39]

ISABELLA   Ay, with such gifts that Heaven shall share with you.

LUCIO   [*aside to her:*] You had marred all else.

ISABELLA   Not with fond sickles of the tested gold,
           Or stones, whose rate are either rich or poor
           As fancy values them; but with true prayers,
           That shall be up at Heaven and enter there
           Ere sun-rise, prayers from preservèd souls,
           From fasting maids, whose minds are dedicate   160

	To nothing temporal.
ANGELO	Well; come to me tomorrow.
LUCIO	[*aside to Isabella:*] Go to; 'tis well; away.
ISABELLA	Heaven keep your Honour safe!
ANGELO	[*aside:*] Amen;
	For I am that way going to temptation
	Where prayers cross.
ISABELLA	At what hour tomorrow
	Shall I attend your lordship?
ANGELO	At any time 'fore noon.
ISABELLA	Save your Honour![40] [*Exeunt all but Angelo.*
ANGELO	From thee; even from thy virtue. 170

What's this, what's this? Is this her fault, or mine?
The tempter or the tempted, who sins most, ha?
Not she; nor doth she tempt; but it is I,
That, lying by the violet in the sun,
Do as the carrion does, not as the flow'r,
Corrupt with virtuous season.[41] Can it be
That modesty may more betray our sense
Than woman's lightness? Having waste ground enough,
Shall we desire to raze the sanctuary,
And pitch our evils there?[42] O, fie, fie, fie!   180
What dost thou, or what art thou, Angelo?
Dost thou desire her foully for those things
That make her good? O, let her brother live:
Thieves for their robbery have authority,
When judges steal themselves. What, do I love her,
That I desire to hear her speak again,
And feast upon her eyes? What is't I dream on?
O cunning enemy, that, to catch a saint,
With saints dost bait thy hook![43] Most dangerous
Is that temptation that doth goad us on   190
To sin in loving virtue. Never could the strumpet,
With all her double vigour, art and nature,
Once stir my temper; but this virtuous maid
Subdues me quite. Ever till now,
When men were fond, I smiled, and wondered how.
                    [*Exit.*

SCENE 3.

Inside a prison.

Enter, separately, the DUKE, *disguised as a friar, and the* PROVOST.

DUKE   Hail to you, Provost! So I think you are.
PROVOST   I am the Provost. What's your will, good friar?
DUKE   Bound by my charity and my blest Order,
          I come to visit the afflicted spirits
          Here in the prison.[44] Do me the common right
          To let me see them, and to make me know
          The nature of their crimes, that I may minister
          To them accordingly.
PROVOST   I would do more than that, if more were needful.

Enter JULIET.

          Look, here comes one: a gentlewoman of mine,   10
          Who, falling in the flaws of her own youth,
          Hath blistered her report. She is with child;
          And he that got it, sentenced: a young man
          More fit to do another such offence
          Than die for this.
DUKE   When must he die?
PROVOST   As I do think, tomorrow.
          [*To Juliet:*] I have provided for you; stay a while,
          And you shall be conducted.
DUKE   Repent you, fair one, of the sin you carry?
JULIET   I do; and bear the shame most patiently.   20
DUKE   I'll teach you how you shall arraign your conscience,
          And try your penitence, if it be sound
          Or hollowly put on.
JULIET   I'll gladly learn.
DUKE   Love you the man that wronged you?
JULIET   Yes, as I love the woman that wronged him.
DUKE   So then, it seems, your most offenceful act
          Was mutually committed.
JULIET   Mutually.
DUKE   Then was your sin of heavier kind than his.[45]

JULIET	I do confess it, and repent it, father.
DUKE	'Tis meet so, daughter; but lest you do repent 30
	As that the sin hath brought you to this shame,
	Which sorrow is always toward ourselves, not Heaven,
	Showing we would not spare Heaven as we love it,
	But as we stand in fear – [46]
JULIET	I do repent me as it is an evil,
	And take the shame with joy.
DUKE	There rest.
	Your partner (as I hear) must die tomorrow,
	And I am going with instruction to him.
	Grace go with you; *benedicite*. [*Exit.* 40
JULIET	'Must die tomorrow'? O injurious love,
	That respites me a life whose very comfort
	Is still a dying horror![47]
PROVOST	'Tis pity of him. [*Exeunt.*

SCENE 4.

A room in the court of justice.

Enter ANGELO.

ANGELO   When I would pray and think, I think and pray
To several subjects: Heaven hath my empty words,
Whilst my invention, hearing not my tongue,
Anchors on Isabel: Heaven in my mouth,
As if I did but only chew His name,
And in my heart the strong and swelling evil
Of my conception. The state whereon I studied
Is, like a good thing being often read,
Grown seared and tedious;[48] yea, my gravity,
Wherein (let no man hear me) I take pride,   10
Could I, with boot, change for an idle plume
Which the air beats for vain. O place, O form,
How often dost thou with thy case, thy habit,
Wrench awe from fools, and tie the wiser souls
To thy false seeming? Blood, thou art blood.
Let's write 'Good Angel' on the Devil's horn;
'Tis not the Devil's crest.[49]

Enter a SERVANT.

                How now? Who's there?
SERVANT   One Isabel, a sister, desires accéss to you.
ANGELO   Teach her the way.   [*Exit servant.*
               O heavens!
Why does my blood thus muster to my heart,   20
Making both it unable for itself
And dispossessing all my other parts
Of necessary fitness?
So play the foolish throngs with one that swoons:
Come all to help him, and so stop the air
By which he should revive; and even so
The general subject to a well-wished king
Quit their own part, and in obsequious fondness
Crowd to his presence, where their untaught love

   Must needs appear offence.

     Enter ISABELLA.

           How now, fair maid? 30

ISABELLA I am come to know your pleasure.

ANGELO That you might know it would much better please me
    Than to demand what 'tis.[50] Your brother cannot live.

ISABELLA Even so. Heaven keep your Honour!

ANGELO Yet may he live a while, and, it may be,
    As long as you or I; yet he must die.

ISABELLA Under your sentence?

ANGELO   Yea.

ISABELLA When?, I beseech you; that in his reprieve
    (Longer or shorter), he may be so fitted
    That his soul sicken not.   40

ANGELO Ha? Fie, these filthy vices! It were as good
    To pardon him that hath from nature stol'n
    A man already made, as to remit
    Their saucy sweetness that do coin Heaven's image
    In stamps that are forbid.[51] 'Tis all as easy
    Falsely to take away a life true-made,
    As to put metal in restrainèd means
    To make a false one.

ISABELLA 'Tis set down so in Heaven, but not in earth.

ANGELO Say you so? Then I shall pose you quickly. 50
    Which had you rather: that the most just law
    Now took your brother's life; or, to redeem him,[52]
    Give up your body to such sweet uncleanness
    As she that he hath stained?

ISABELLA   Sir, believe this:
    I had rather give my body than my soul.

ANGELO I talk not of your soul; our compelled sins
    Stand more for number than for accompt.[53]

ISABELLA   How say you?

ANGELO Nay, I'll not warrant that; for I can speak
    Against the thing I say. Answer to this:
    I (now the voice of the recorded law) 60
    Pronounce a sentence on your brother's life;
    Might there not be a charity in sin

	To save this brother's life?	
ISABELLA	Please you to do't,	

        To save this brother's life?
ISABELLA   Please you to do't,
        I'll take it, as a peril to my soul,
        It is no sin at all, but charity.
ANGELO   Pleased you to do't, at peril of your soul,
        Were equal poise of sin and charity.
ISABELLA That I do beg his life, if it be sin,
        Heaven let me bear it; you granting of my suit,
        If that be sin, I'll make it my morn prayer   70
        To have it added to the faults of mine,
        And nothing of your answer.
ANGELO   Nay, but hear me;
        Your sense pursues not mine; either you are ignorant,
        Or seem so, craftily; and that's not good.
ISABELLA Let me be ignorant, and in nothing good[54]
        But graciously to know I am no better.
ANGELO   Thus wisdom wishes to appear most bright,
        When it doth tax itself; as these black masks
        Proclaim an enshield beauty ten times louder
        Than beauty could, displayed. But mark me: 80
        To be receivèd plain, I'll speak more gross.
        Your brother is to die.
ISABELLA So.
ANGELO   And his offence is so, as it appears,
        Accountant to the law upon that pain.
ISABELLA True.
ANGELO   Admit no other way to save his life
        (As I subscribe not that, nor any other),
        But, in the loss of question,[55] that you, his sister,
        Finding yourself desired of such a person   90
        Whose credit with the judge, or own great place,
        Could fetch your brother from the manacles
        Of the all-binding law, and that there were
        No earthly mean to save him but that either
        You must lay down the treasures of your body
        To this supposed, or else to let him suffer:
        What would you do?
ISABELLA As much for my poor brother as myself;
        That is: were I under the terms of death,

	Th'impression of keen whips I'd wear as rubies, 100
	And strip myself to death as to a bed
	That longing have been sick for, ere I'd yield
	My body up to shame.

ANGELO   Then must your brother die.

ISABELLA And 'twere the cheaper way:
          Better it were a brother died at once
          Than that a sister, by redeeming him,
          Should die for ever.[56]

ANGELO   Were not you then as cruel as the sentence
          That you have slandered so?   110

ISABELLA Ignomy in ransom and free pardon
          Are of two houses: lawful mercy
          Is nothing kin to foul redemption.

ANGELO   You seemed of late to make the law a tyrant,
          And rather proved the sliding of your brother
          A merriment than a vice.

ISABELLA O pardon me, my lord; it oft falls out,
          To have what we would have,
          We speak not what we mean:
          I something do excuse the thing I hate   120
          For his advantage that I dearly love.

ANGELO   We are all frail.

ISABELLA   Else let my brother die,
          If not a fedary but only he
          Owe and succeed thy weakness.

ANGELO   Nay, women are frail too.

ISABELLA Ay, as the glasses where they view themselves,
          Which are as easy broke as they make forms.
          Women? Help, Heaven! Men their creation mar
          In profiting by them. Nay, call us ten times frail;
          For we are soft as our complexions are,   130
          And credulous to false prints.[57]

ANGELO   I think it well;
          And from this testimony of your own sex
          (Since I suppose we are made to be no stronger
          Than faults may shake our frames),[58] let me be bold:
          I do arrest your words. Be that you are,
          That is, a woman; if you be more, you're none;

If you be one (as you are well expressed
By all external warrants), show it now
By putting on the destined livery.

ISABELLA   I have no tongue but one; gentle my lord,   140
Let me entreat you speak the former language.

ANGELO   Plainly conceive, I love you.

ISABELLA   My brother did love Juliet,
And you tell me that he shall die for't.

ANGELO   He shall not, Isabel, if you give me love.

ISABELLA   I know your virtue hath a license in't,
Which seems a little fouler than it is,
To pluck on others.

ANGELO   Believe me, on mine honour,
My words express my purpose.

ISABELLA   Ha? Little honour, to be much believed,   150
And most pernicious purpose! Seeming, seeming!
I will proclaim thee, Angelo, look for't.
Sign me a present pardon for my brother,
Or, with an outstretched throat, I'll tell the world aloud
What man thou art.

ANGELO   Who will believe thee, Isabel?
My unsoiled name, th'austereness of my life,
My vouch against you, and my place i'th'state,
Will so your accusation overweigh
That you shall stifle in your own report,
And smell of calumny.[59] I have begun,   160
And now I give my sensual race the rein:
Fit thy consent to my sharp appetite;
Lay by all nicety and prolixious blushes
That banish what they sue for; redeem thy brother
By yielding up thy body to my will;
Or else he must not only die the death,
But thy unkindness shall his death draw out
To ling'ring sufferance. Answer me tomorrow,
Or, by the affection that now guides me most,
I'll prove a tyrant to him. As for you,   170
Say what you can; my false o'erweighs your true.[*Exit.*

ISABELLA   To whom should I complain? Did I tell this,
Who would believe me? O perilous mouths,

That bear in them one and the self-same tongue,
Either of condemnation or approof,
Bidding the law make curtsy to their will;
Hooking both right and wrong to th'appetite,
To follow as it draws! I'll to my brother.
Though he hath fall'n by prompture of the blood,
Yet hath he in him such a mind of honour   180
That, had he twenty heads to tender down
On twenty bloody blocks, he'd yield them up
Before his sister should her body stoop
To such abhorred pollution.
Then, Isabel, live chaste, and brother, die:
More than our brother is our chastity.
I'll tell him yet of Angelo's request,
And fit his mind to death, for his soul's rest.   [*Exit.*

ACT 3, SCENE 1.

Inside the prison.

Enter the DUKE *(still disguised as a friar),* CLAUDIO *and the* PROVOST.

DUKE   So then you hope of pardon from Lord Angelo?

CLAUDIO   The miserable have no other medicine
            But only hope:
            I've hope to live, and am prepared to die.

DUKE   Be absolute for death: either death or life
            Shall thereby be the sweeter. Reason thus with life:
            If I do lose thee, I do lose a thing
            That none but fools would keep: a breath thou art,
            Servile to all the skyey influences
            That dost this habitation, where thou keep'st,   10
            Hourly afflict. Merely, thou art Death's fool;
            For him thou labour'st by thy flight to shun,
            And yet run'st toward him still. Thou art not noble,
            For all th'accommodations that thou bear'st
            Are nursed by baseness.[60] Thou'rt by no means valiant,
            For thou dost fear the soft and tender fork
            Of a poor worm. Thy best of rest is sleep,
            And that thou oft provok'st; yet grossly fear'st
            Thy death, which is no more.[61] Thou art not thyself,
            For thou exists on many a thousand grains   20
            That issue out of dust. Happy thou art not;
            For, what thou hast not, still thou striv'st to get,
            And what thou hast, forget'st. Thou art not certain,
            For thy complexion shifts to strange effects,
            After the moon.[62] If thou art rich, thou'rt poor;
            For, like an ass whose back with ingots bows,
            Thou bear'st thy heavy riches but a journey,
            And Death unloads thee. Friend hast thou none;
            For thine own bowels which do call thee 'Sire',
            The mere effusion of thy proper loins,   30
            Do curse the gout, sapego and the rheum
            For ending thee no sooner.[63] Thou hast nor youth nor age,

But, as it were, an after-dinner's sleep,
Dreaming on both; for all thy blessèd youth
Becomes as agèd, and doth beg the alms
Of palsied eld; and when thou art old and rich,
Thou hast neither heat, affection, limb, nor beauty,
To make thy riches pleasant. What's yet in this
That bears the name of life? Yet in this life
Lie hid moe thousand deaths; yet death we fear,   40
That makes these odds all even.

CLAUDIO   I humbly thank you.
To sue to live, I find I seek to die,
And, seeking death, find life.[64] Let it come on.

ISABELLA   [beyond:] What ho! Peace here; grace and good
                                  company!

PROVOST   Who's there? Come in; the wish deserves a welcome.

DUKE   [to Claudio:] Dear sir, ere long I'll visit you again.

CLAUDIO   Most holy sir, I thank you.

Enter ISABELLA.

ISABELLA   My business is a word or two with Claudio.

PROVOST   And very welcome. – Look, signor, here's your sister.

DUKE   [aside to Provost:] Provost, a word with you.   50

PROVOST   As many as you please.   [Duke and Provost move aside.

DUKE   Bring me to hear them speak, where I may be concealed.
                       [Exeunt Duke and Provost.

CLAUDIO   Now, sister, what's the comfort?

ISABELLA   Why, as all comforts are: most good, most good, indeed.
Lord Angelo, having affairs to Heaven,
Intends you for his swift ambassador,
Where you shall be an everlasting leiger.
Therefore, your best appointment make with speed:
Tomorrow you set on.

CLAUDIO   Is there no remedy?   60

ISABELLA   None, but such remedy as, to save a head,
To cleave a heart in twain.

CLAUDIO   But is there any?

ISABELLA   Yes, brother, you may live:
There is a devilish mercy in the judge,
If you'll implore it, that will free your life,

But fetter you till death.

CLAUDIO   Perpetual durance?

ISABELLA Ay, just; perpetual durance: a restraint,
          Though all the world's vastidity you had,
          To a determined scope.

CLAUDIO   But in what nature?

ISABELLA In such a one as, you consenting to't,   70
          Would bark your honour from that trunk you bear,
          And leave you naked.

CLAUDIO   Let me know the point.

ISABELLA O, I do fear thee, Claudio; and I quake,
          Lest thou a feverous life shouldst entertain,
          And six or seven winters more respect
          Than a perpetual honour. Dar'st thou die?
          The sense of death is most in apprehension;
          And the poor beetle that we tread upon,
          In corporal sufferance finds a pang as great
          As when a giant dies.[65]   80

CLAUDIO   Why give you me this shame?
          Think you I can a resolution fetch
          From flow'ry tenderness? If I must die,
          I will encounter darkness as a bride,
          And hug it in mine arms.

ISABELLA There spake my brother; there my father's grave
          Did utter forth a voice. Yes, thou must die:
          Thou art too noble to conserve a life
          In base appliances. This outward-sainted deputy,
          Whose settled visage and deliberate word   90
          Nips youth i'th'head, and follies doth enmew
          As falcon doth the fowl,[66] is yet a devil:
          His filth within being cast, he would appear
          A pond as deep as Hell.

CLAUDIO   The princely Angelo?[67]

ISABELLA O, 'tis the cunning livery of Hell,
          The damnèd'st body to invest and cover
          In princely guards! Dost thou think, Claudio,
          If I would yield him my virginity,
          Thou mightst be freed?

CLAUDIO   O heavens! It cannot be.   100

ISABELLA   Yes, he would give't thee, from this rank offence,
            So to offend him still.[68] This night's the time
            That I should do what I abhor to name,
            Or else thou diest tomorrow.

CLAUDIO   Thou shalt not do't.

ISABELLA   O, were it but my life,
            I'd throw it down for your deliverance
            As frankly as a pin.

CLAUDIO   Thanks, dear Isabel.

ISABELLA   Be ready, Claudio, for your death tomorrow.

CLAUDIO   Yes . . . Has he affections in him,   110
            That thus can make him bite the law by th'nose
            When he would force it? Sure it is no sin,
            Or of the deadly seven it is the least.[69]

ISABELLA   Which is the least?

CLAUDIO   If it were damnable, he being so wise,
            Why would he for the momentary trick
            Be pérdurably fined? O Isabel!

ISABELLA   What says my brother?

CLAUDIO   Death is a fearful thing.

ISABELLA   And shamèd life a hateful.

CLAUDIO   Ay, but to die, and go we know not where;   120
            To lie in cold obstruction, and to rot;
            This sensible warm motion to become
            A kneaded clod; and the delighted spirit
            To bathe in fiery floods, or to reside
            In thrilling regions of thick-ribbèd ice;
            To be imprisoned in the viewless winds,
            And blown with restless violence round about
            The pendent world; or to be worse than worst
            Of those that lawless and incertain thoughts
            Imagine howling: 'tis too horrible!   130
            The weariest and most loathèd worldly life
            That age, ache, penury and imprisonment
            Can lay on nature is a Paradise
            To what we fear of death.[70]

ISABELLA   Alas, alas!

CLAUDIO   Sweet sister, let me live!
            What sin you do to save a brother's life,

Nature dispenses with the deed so far
That it becomes a virtue.

ISABELLA   O you beast!
O faithless coward, O dishonest wretch!
Wilt thou be made a man out of my vice?   140
Is't not a kind of incest, to take life
From thine own sister's shame? What should I think?
Heaven shield my mother played my father fair:
For such a warpèd slip of wilderness
Ne'er issued from his blood.[71] Take my defiance;
Die, perish! Might but my bending down
Reprieve thee from thy fate, it should proceed.
I'll pray a thousand prayers for thy death,
No word to save thee.

CLAUDIO   Nay, hear me, Isabel –
ISABELLA   O fie, fie, fie!   150
Thy sin's not accidental, but a trade.
Mercy to thee would prove itself a bawd;
'Tis best that thou diest quickly.

CLAUDIO   O, hear me, Isabella!

                    Enter the DUKE *(as friar).*

DUKE   Vouchsafe a word, young sister, but one word.
ISABELLA   What is your will?
DUKE   Might you dispense with your leisure, I would by and
            by have some speech with you; the satisfaction I
            would require is likewise your own benefit.
ISABELLA   I have no superfluous leisure; my stay must be stolen   160
            out of other affairs; but I will attend you a while.
                    [She waits aside, out of earshot.
DUKE   Son, I have overheard what hath passed between you
            and your sister. Angelo had never the purpose to cor-
            rupt her; only, he hath made an assay of her virtue, to
            practise his judgement with the disposition of natures.
            She (having the truth of honour in her) hath made him
            that gracious denial which he is most glad to receive. I
            am confessor to Angelo, and I know this to be true;
            therefore prepare yourself to death. Do not satisfy your
            resolution with hopes that are fallible; tomorrow you   170

must die; go to your knees and make ready.

CLAUDIO   Let me ask my sister pardon. I am so out of love with life that I will sue to be rid of it.

DUKE   Hold you there. Farewell.   [*Claudio joins Isabella.* [*Duke calls:*] Provost, a word with you.

Enter the PROVOST.

PROVOST   What's your will, father?

DUKE   That, now you are come, you will be gone. Leave me a while with the maid. My mind promises with my habit, no loss shall touch her by my company.

PROVOST   In good time.[72]   [*Exit Provost with Claudio.*   180

DUKE   – The hand that hath made you fair hath made you good; the goodness that is cheap in beauty makes beauty brief in goodness; but grace, being the soul of your complexion, shall keep the body of it ever fair.[73] The assault that Angelo hath made to you, fortune hath conveyed to my understanding; and, but that frailty hath examples for his falling, I should wonder at Angelo. How will you do to content this substitute, and to save your brother?

ISABELLA   I am now going to resolve him: I had rather my brother   190 die by the law than my son should be unlawfully born. But, O, how much is the good Duke deceived in Angelo! If ever he return, and I can speak to him, I will open my lips in vain, or discover his government.

DUKE   That shall not be much amiss; yet, as the matter now stands, he will avoid your accusation: he made trial of you only. Therefore fasten your ear on my advisings; to the love I have in doing good, a remedy presents itself. I do make myself believe that you may most upright- eously do a poor wronged lady a merited benefit; redeem   200 your brother from the angry law; do no stain to your own gracious person; and much please the absent Duke, if peradventure he shall ever return to have hearing of this business.

ISABELLA   Let me hear you speak farther; I have spirit to do anything that appears not foul in the truth of my spirit.

DUKE   Virtue is bold, and goodness never fearful. Have you

not heard speak of Mariana, the sister of Frederick, the
great soldier who miscarried at sea?

ISABELLA I have heard of the lady, and good words went with   210
          her name.

DUKE   She should this Angelo have married; was affianced to
          her by oath, and the nuptial appointed; between
          which time of the contract and limit of the solemnity,
          her brother Frederick was wracked at sea, having in
          that perished vessel the dowry of his sister. But mark
          how heavily this befell to the poor gentlewoman: there
          she lost a noble and renowned brother, in his love
          toward her ever most kind and natural; with him, the
          portion and sinew of her fortune, her marriage-dowry;   220
          with both, her combinate husband, this well-seeming
          Angelo.

ISABELLA Can this be so? Did Angelo so leave her?

DUKE   Left her in her tears, and dried not one of them with
          his comfort; swallowed his vows whole, pretending, in
          her, discoveries of dishonour; in few, bestowed her on
          her own lamentation, which she yet wears for his sake;
          and he, a marble to her tears, is washed with them, but
          relents not.

ISABELLA What a merit were it in death to take this poor maid   230
          from the world! What corruption in this life, that it will
          let this man live! But how out of this can she avail?

DUKE   It is a rupture that you may easily heal; and the cure of
          it not only saves your brother, but keeps you from
          dishonour in doing it.

ISABELLA Show me how, good father.

DUKE   This forenamed maid hath yet in her the continuance
          of her first affection: his unjust unkindness (that in all
          reason should have quenched her love) hath (like an
          impediment in the current) made it more violent and   240
          unruly. Go you to Angelo; answer his requiring with a
          plausible obedience; agree with his demands to the
          point; only refer yourself to this advantage: first, that
          your stay with him may not be long; that the place may
          have all shadow and silence in it; and the time answer
          to convenience.[74] This being granted in course, and

now follows all: we shall advise this wronged maid to
stead up your appointment, go in your place. If the
encounter acknowledge itself hereafter, it may compel
him to her recompense; and here, by this, is your 250
brother saved, your honour untainted, the poor
Mariana advantaged, and the corrupt deputy scaled.
The maid will I·frame and make fit for his attempt. If
you think well to carry this as you may, the doubleness
of the benefit defends the deceit from reproof. What
think you of it?

ISABELLA   The image of it gives me content already, and I trust it
will grow to a most prosperous perfection.

DUKE   It lies much in your holding up. Haste you speedily to
Angelo; if for this night he entreat you to his bed, give 260
him promise of satisfaction. I will presently to Saint
Luke's; there, at the moated grange, resides this dejected
Mariana. At that place call upon me; and dispatch with
Angelo, that it may be quickly.

ISABELLA   I thank you for this comfort. Fare you well, good
father.   [*Exeunt separately.*

SCENE 2.[75]

A street near the prison.

Enter, on one side, the DUKE *(disguised as friar);*
on the other, ELBOW *and* OFFICERS *with* POMPEY.

ELBOW   [*to Pompey:*] Nay, if there be no remedy for it, but that
you will needs buy and sell men and women like
beasts, we shall have all the world drink brown and
white bastard.[76]

DUKE   O heavens, what stuff is here?

POMPEY   'Twas never merry world since, of two usuries, the
merriest was put down, and the worser allowed by order
of law a furred gown to keep him warm; and furred with
fox on lamb-skins too, to signify that craft, being richer
than innocency, stands for the facing.[77]   10

ELBOW   Come your way, sir. – Bless you, good father friar.[78]

DUKE   And you, good brother father. What offence hath this
man made you, sir?

ELBOW   Marry, sir, he hath offended the law; and, sir, we take
him to be a thief too, sir, for we have found upon him,
sir, a strange pick-lock, which we have sent to the
deputy.

DUKE   [*to Pompey:*] Fie, sirrah, a bawd, a wicked bawd!
The evil that thou causest to be done,
That is thy means to live. Do thou but think   20
What 'tis to cram a maw or clothe a back
From such a filthy vice: say to thyself,
'From their abominable and beastly touches
I drink, I eat, array myself, and live.'
Canst thou believe thy living is a life,
So stinkingly depending? Go mend, go mend.

POMPEY   Indeed, it does stink in some sort, sir; but yet, sir,
I would prove –

DUKE   Nay, if the Devil have given thee proofs for sin,
Thou wilt prove his.[79] – Take him to prison, officer;   30
Correction and instruction must both work

Ere this rude beast will profit.

ELBOW   He must before the deputy, sir; he has given him
         warning. The deputy cannot abide a whoremaster; if he
         be a whoremonger, and comes before him, he were as
         good go a mile on his errand.

DUKE   That we were all, as some would seem to be,
         From our faults, as his faults from seeming, free.

ELBOW   His neck will come to your waist: a cord, sir.[80]

Enter LUCIO.

POMPEY   I spy comfort; I cry bail! Here's a gentleman, and a   40
         friend of mine.

LUCIO   How now, noble Pompey! What, at the wheels of
         Cæsar? Art thou led in triumph? What, is there none
         of Pygmalion's images, newly made woman, to be had
         now for putting the hand in the pocket and extracting
         clutched? What reply? Ha? What say'st thou to this
         tune, matter, and method? Is't not drowned i'th'last
         rain? Ha? What say'st thou, trot? Is the world as it was,
         man? Which is the way? Is it sad, and few words? Or
         how? The trick of it?[81]   50

DUKE   Still thus, and thus; still worse!

LUCIO   How doth my dear morsel, thy mistress? Procures she
         still? Ha?

POMPEY   Troth, sir, she hath eaten up all her beef, and she is
         herself in the tub.[82]

LUCIO   Why, 'tis good: it is the right of it; it must be so. Ever
         your fresh whore and your powdered bawd, an
         unshunned consequence; it must be so. Art going to
         prison, Pompey?

POMPEY   Yes, faith, sir.   60

LUCIO   Why, 'tis not amiss, Pompey. Farewell; go, say I sent
         thee thither. For debt, Pompey? Or how?

ELBOW   For being a bawd, for being a bawd.

LUCIO   Well, then, imprison him. If imprisonment be the due
         of a bawd, why, 'tis his right. Bawd is he doubtless, and
         of antiquity, too; bawd born. Farewell, good Pompey.
         Commend me to the prison, Pompey. You will turn
         good husband now, Pompey; you will keep the house.

POMPEY	I hope, sir, your good Worship will be my bail.
LUCIO	No, indeed will I not, Pompey; it is not the wear. I 70 will pray, Pompey, to increase your bondage. If you take it not patiently, why, your mettle is the more.[83] Adieu, trusty Pompey. – Bless you, friar.
DUKE	And you.
LUCIO	Does Bridget paint still, Pompey? Ha?
ELBOW	[to Pompey:] Come your ways, sir; come.
POMPEY	[to Lucio:] You will not bail me then, sir?
LUCIO	Then, Pompey, nor now.[84] – What news abroad, friar? What news?
ELBOW	Come your ways, sir; come. 80
LUCIO	Go to kennel, Pompey, go.

                         [*Exeunt Elbow, Pompey and officers.*

	What news, friar, of the Duke?
DUKE	I know none: can you tell me of any?
LUCIO	Some say he is with the Emperor of Russia; other some, he is in Rome; but where is he, think you?
DUKE	I know not where; but wheresoever, I wish him well.
LUCIO	It was a mad fantastical trick of him to steal from the state, and usurp the beggary he was never born to. Lord Angelo dukes it well in his absence; he puts trans- gression to't. 90
DUKE	He does well in't.
LUCIO	A little more lenity to lechery would do no harm in him; something too crabbed that way, friar.
DUKE	It is too general a vice, and severity must cure it.
LUCIO	Yes, in good sooth, the vice is of a great kindred; it is well allied; but it is impossible to extirp it quite, friar, till eating and drinking be put down. They say this Angelo was not made by man and woman after this downright way of creation: is it true, think you?
DUKE	How should he be made, then? 100
LUCIO	Some report a sea-maid spawned him; some, that he was begot between two stock-fishes. But it is certain that when he makes water, his urine is congealed ice; that I know to be true. And he is a motion ungenerative; that's infallible.
DUKE	You are pleasant, sir, and speak apace.[85]

LUCIO   Why, what a ruthless thing is this in him, for the rebel-
         lion of a cod-piece to take away the life of a man! Would
         the Duke that is absent have done this? Ere he would
         have hanged a man for the getting a hundred bastards,   110
         he would have paid for the nursing a thousand. He had
         some feeling of the sport; he knew the service, and that
         instructed him to mercy.

DUKE   I never heard the absent Duke much detected for
         women; he was not inclined that way.

LUCIO   O sir, you are deceived.

DUKE   'Tis not possible.

LUCIO   Who, not the Duke? Yes, your beggar of fifty; and his
         use was to put a ducat in her clack-dish. The Duke had
         crotchets in him. He would be drunk too; that let me   120
         inform you.

DUKE   You do him wrong, surely.

LUCIO   Sir, I was an inward of his. A shy fellow was the Duke;
         and I believe I know the cause of his withdrawing.

DUKE   What, I prithee, might be the cause?

LUCIO   No, pardon; 'tis a secret must be locked within the
         teeth and the lips; but this I can let you understand: the
         greater file of the subject held the Duke to be wise.

DUKE   Wise? Why, no question but he was.

LUCIO   A very superficial, ignorant, unweighing fellow.   130

DUKE   Either this is envy in you, folly, or mistaking! The very
         stream of his life, and the business he hath helmed, must,
         upon a warranted need, give him a better proclamation.
         Let him be but testimonied in his own bringings-forth,
         and he shall appear to the envious a scholar, a statesman,
         and a soldier. Therefore you speak unskilfully; or, if
         your knowledge be more, it is much darkened in your
         malice.

LUCIO   Sir, I know him, and I love him.

DUKE   Love talks with better knowledge, and knowledge   140
         with dearer love.[86]

LUCIO   Come, sir, I know what I know.

DUKE   I can hardly believe that, since you know not what
         you speak. But, if ever the Duke return, as our prayers
         are he may, let me desire you to make your answer

	before him. If it be honest you have spoke, you have courage to maintain it. I am bound to call upon you; and I pray you, your name?
LUCIO	Sir, my name is Lucio, well known to the Duke.
DUKE	He shall know you better, sir, if I may live to report you.

150

LUCIO   I fear you not.

DUKE   O, you hope the Duke will return no more; or you imagine me too unhurtful an opposite. But, indeed, I can do you little harm: you'll forswear this again.

LUCIO   I'll be hanged first. Thou art deceived in me, friar. But no more of this. Canst thou tell if Claudio die tomorrow or no?

DUKE   Why should he die, sir?

LUCIO   Why? For filling a bottle with a tun-dish. I would the Duke we talk of were returned again. This ungenitured agent will unpeople the province with continency. Sparrows must not build in his house-eaves, because they are lecherous. The Duke yet would have dark deeds darkly answered; he would never bring them to light. Would he were returned! Marry, this Claudio is condemned for untrussing. Farewell, good friar; I prithee pray for me. The Duke (I say to thee again) would eat mutton on Fridays.[87] He's now past it: yet (and I say to thee) he would mouth with a beggar, though she smelt brown bread and garlic. Say that I said so. Farewell.

160

170

                                                        [*Exit.*

DUKE   No might nor greatness in mortality
Can censure scape; back-wounding calumny
The whitest virtue strikes. What king so strong
Can tie the gall up in the slanderous tongue?
– But who comes here?

Enter ESCALUS, *the* PROVOST, *and* OFFICERS *with* MISTRESS OVERDONE.

ESCALUS   Go, away with her to prison.

OVERDONE Good my lord, be good to me; your Honour is accounted a merciful man; good my lord.

ESCALUS   Double and treble admonition, and still forfeit in the same kind? This would make mercy swear and play the tyrant.

180

PROVOST   A bawd of eleven years' continuance, may it please your Honour.

OVERDONE   My lord, this is one Lucio's information against me. Mistress Kate Keepdown was with child by him in the Duke's time; he promised her marriage. His child is a year and a quarter old come Philip and Jacob;[88] I have kept it myself; and see how he goes about to abuse me.

ESCALUS   That fellow is a fellow of much license: let him be   190
called before us. Away with her to prison. – Go to; no
more words.   [*Exeunt officers with Mistress Overdone.*
Provost, my brother Angelo will not be altered: Claudio
must die tomorrow. Let him be furnished with divines,
and have all charitable preparation. If my brother
wrought by my pity, it should not be so with him.

PROVOST   So please you, this friar hath been with him, and
advised him for th'entertainment of death.
                             [*Exeunt Provost and Overdone.*

ESCALUS   Good even, good father.

DUKE   Bliss and goodness on you.   200

ESCALUS   Of whence are you?

DUKE   Not of this country, though my chance is now
To use it for my time: I am a brother
Of gracious Order, late come from the See,
In special business from his Holiness.

ESCALUS   What news abroad i'th'world?

DUKE   None, but that there is so great a fever on goodness
that the dissolution of it must cure it. Novelty is only
in request; and, as it is, as dangerous to be agèd in any
kind of course as it is virtuous to be inconstant in any   210
undertaking.[89] There is scarce truth enough alive to
make societies secure, but security enough to make
fellowships accursed. Much upon this riddle runs the
wisdom of the world. This news is old enough, yet it is
every day's news. I pray you, sir, of what disposition
was the Duke?

ESCALUS   One that, above all other strifes, contended especially
to know himself.

DUKE   What pleasure was he given to?

ESCALUS   Rather rejoicing to see another merry, than merry at   220

anything which professed to make him rejoice. A gentleman of all temperance. But leave we him to his events,
with a prayer they may prove prosperous, and let me
desire to know how you find Claudio prepared. I am
made to understand that you have lent him visitation.

DUKE He professes to have received no sinister measure from
his judge, but most willingly humbles himself to the
determination of justice. Yet had he framed to himself
(by the instruction of his frailty) many deceiving promises
of life, which I (by my good leisure) have discredited to   230
him, and now he is resolved to die.

ESCALUS You have paid the heavens your function, and the
prisoner the very debt of your calling.[90] I have laboured
for the poor gentleman to the extremest shore of my
modesty, but my brother justice have I found so severe
that he hath forced me to tell him he is indeed Justice.[91]

DUKE If his own life answer the straitness of his proceeding,
it shall become him well; wherein if he chance to fail,
he hath sentenced himself.

ESCALUS I am going to visit the prisoner. Fare you well.   240
DUKE Peace be with you.   [Exit Escalus.
He who the sword of Heaven will bear
Should be as holy as severe:
Pattern in himself to know,
Grace to stand, and virtue go;
More nor less to others paying
Than by self-offences weighing.[92]
Shame to him whose cruel striking
Kills for faults of his own liking!
Twice treble shame on Angelo,   250
To weed my vice and let his grow!
O, what may man within him hide,
Though angel on the outward side?
How may likeness, made in crimes,
Making practice on the times,
To draw with idle spiders' strings
Most ponderous and substantial things?[93]
Craft against vice I must apply.
With Angelo tonight shall lie

His old betrothèd (but despised);   260
So disguise shall, by th'disguised,
Pay with falsehood false exacting,
And perform an old contracting.[94]   [*Exit.*

ACT 4, SCENE 1.

Inside the moated grange.

Enter MARIANA *and a singing* BOY.[95]

BOY *sings:*

> Take, O take those lips away,
>   That so sweetly were forsworn;
> And those eyes, the break-of-day
>   Lights that do mislead the morn;[96]
> But my kisses bring again, bring again;
> Seals of love, but sealed in vain, sealed in vain.

Enter the DUKE *(disguised as friar).*

MARIANA Break off thy song, and haste thee quick away;
Here comes a man of comfort, whose advice
Hath often stilled my brawling discontent.   [*Exit boy.*
– I cry you mercy, sir, and well could wish   10
You had not found me here so musical.
Let me excuse me, and believe me so,
My mirth it much displeased, but pleased my woe.

DUKE   'Tis good; though music oft hath such a charm,
To make bad good, and good provoke to harm.
I pray you tell me, hath anybody enquired for me here
today? Much upon this time have I promised here to
meet.

MARIANA You have not been enquired after; I have sat here all day.

Enter ISABELLA.

DUKE   I do constantly believe you: the time is come even   20
now. I shall crave your forbearance a little; may be I
will call upon you anon, for some advantage to yourself.

MARIANA I am always bound to you.   [*Exit Mariana.*

DUKE   – Very well met, and welcome.
What is the news from this good deputy?

ISABELLA He hath a garden circummured with brick,
Whose western side is with a vineyard backed;
And to that vineyard is a planchèd gate

That makes his opening with this bigger key;
This other doth command a little door,   30
Which from the vineyard to the garden leads.
There have I made my promise
Upon the heavy middle of the night
To call upon him.

DUKE   But shall you on your knowledge find this way?

ISABELLA   I have ta'en a due and wary note upon't.
With whispering and most guilty diligence,
In action all of precept, he did show me
The way twice o'er.

DUKE   Are there no other tokens
Between you 'greed, concerning her observance?   40

ISABELLA   No, none, but only a repair i'th'dark;
And that I have possessed him my most stay
Can be but brief; for I have made him know
I have a servant comes with me along,
That stays upon me; whose persuasion is
I come about my brother.

DUKE   'Tis well borne up.
I have not yet made known to Mariana
A word of this. – What ho, within! Come forth.

Enter MARIANA.

I pray you be acquainted with this maid;
She comes to do you good.   50

ISABELLA   I do desire the like.

DUKE   [*to Mariana:*] Do you persuade yourself that I respect you?

MARIANA   Good friar, I know you do, and have found it.[97]

DUKE   Take, then, this your companion by the hand,
Who hath a story ready for your ear.
I shall attend your leisure, but make haste:
The vaporous night approaches.

MARIANA   [*to Isabella:*] Will't please you walk aside?

[Exeunt Mariana and Isabella.

DUKE   O place and greatness! Millions of false eyes
Are stuck upon thee; volumes of report   60
Run with these false and most contrarious quests
Upon thy doings; thousand escapes of wit

Make thee the father of their idle dream,
And rack thee in their fancies.[98]

    Enter MARIANA *and* ISABELLA.

  – Welcome, how agreed?

ISABELLA   She'll take the enterprise upon her, father,
If you advise it.

DUKE   It is not my consent,
But my entreaty too.

ISABELLA   [*to Mariana:*] Little have you to say,
When you depart from him, but, soft and low,   70
'Remember now my brother.'

MARIANA   Fear me not.

DUKE   Nor, gentle daughter, fear you not at all.
He is your husband on a pre-contract.
To bring you thus together 'tis no sin,
Sith that the justice of your title to him
Doth flourish the deceit. Come, let us go;
Our corn's to reap, for yet our tithe's to sow.[99]

             [*Exeunt.*

SCENE 2.

Inside the prison.

Enter the PROVOST *and* POMPEY.

PROVOST Come hither, sirrah. Can you cut off a man's head?

POMPEY If the man be a bachelor, sir, I can; but if he be a
    married man, he's his wife's head, and I can never cut
    of a woman's head.[100]

PROVOST Come sir, leave me your snatches, and yield me a direct
    answer. Tomorrow morning are to die Claudio and
    Barnardine. Here is in our prison a common execu-
    tioner, who in his office lacks a helper. If you will take it
    on you to assist him, it shall redeem you from your gyves;
    if not, you shall have your full time of imprisonment,   10
    and your deliverance with an unpitied whipping, for
    you have been a notorious bawd.

POMPEY Sir, I have been an unlawful bawd time out of mind,
    but yet I will be content to be a lawful hangman. I
    would be glad to receive some instructions from my
    fellow partner.

PROVOST – What ho, Abhorson! Where's Abhorson there?

Enter ABHORSON.

ABHOR. Do you call, sir?

PROVOST Sirrah, here's a fellow will help you tomorrow in your
    execution. If you think it meet, compound with him   20
    by the year, and let him abide here with you; if not,
    use him for the present, and dismiss him. He cannot
    plead his estimation with you: he hath been a bawd.

ABHOR. A bawd, sir? Fie upon him! He will discredit our
    mystery.

PROVOST Go to, sir; you weigh equally: a feather will turn the
    scale.   [*Exit Provost.*

POMPEY Pray, sir, by your good favour – for surely, sir, a good
    favour you have, but that you have a hanging look – do
    you call, sir, your occupation 'a mystery'?   30

ABHOR. Ay sir, a mystery.

POMPEY   Painting, sir, I have heard say, is a mystery; and your
           whores, sir, being members of my occupation, using
           painting, do prove my occupation a mystery; but what
           mystery there should be in hanging, if I should be
           hanged, I cannot imagine.

ABHOR.   Sir, it *is* a mystery.

POMPEY   Proof?

ABHOR.   Every true man's apparel fits your thief.

POMPEY   If it be too little for your thief, your true man thinks it   40
           big enough; if it be too big for your thief, your thief
           thinks it little enough. So every true man's apparel fits
           your thief.[101]

                        Enter the PROVOST.

PROVOST   Are you agreed?

POMPEY   Sir, I will serve him; for I do find your hangman is a
           more penitent trade than your bawd: he doth oftener
           ask forgiveness.[102]

PROVOST   [*to Abhorson:*] You, sirrah, provide your block and your
           axe tomorrow four o'clock.

ABHOR.   Come on, bawd. I will instruct thee in my trade; follow.   50

POMPEY   I do desire to learn, sir; and I hope, if you have
           occasion to use me for your own turn, you shall find
           me yare. For truly, sir, for your kindness, I owe you a
           good turn.[103]

PROVOST   Call hither Barnardine and Claudio.
                              [*Exeunt Abhorson and Pompey.*
           Th'one has my pity; not a jot the other,
           Being a murtherer, though he were my brother.

                        Enter CLAUDIO.

           Look, here's the warrant, Claudio, for thy death.
           'Tis now dead midnight, and by eight tomorrow
           Thou must be made immortal. Where's Barnardine?   60

CLAUDIO   As fast locked up in sleep as guiltless labour
           When it lies starkly in the traveller's bones.
           He will not wake.

PROVOST   Who can do good on him?
           Well, go, prepare yourself. [*Knocking heard.*] But
                              hark, what noise?

Heaven give your spirits comfort!   [*Exit Claudio.*
[*Knocking continues.*]   By and by!
– I hope it is some pardon or reprieve
For the most gentle Claudio.

    Enter the DUKE *(disguised as friar).*

                          Welcome, father.

DUKE   The best and wholesom'st spirits of the night
Envelop you, good Provost! Who called here of late?
PROVOST None, since the curfew rung.
DUKE   Not Isabel?
PROVOST   No.   70
DUKE   They will then, ere't be long.
PROVOST What comfort is for Claudio?
DUKE   There's some in hope.
PROVOST   It is a bitter deputy.
DUKE   Not so, not so: his life is paralleled
Even with the stroke and line of his great justice;
He doth with holy abstinence subdue
That in himself which he spurs on his pow'r
To qualify in others. Were he mealed with that
Which he corrects, then were he tyrannous;
But this being so, he's just. [*Knocking heard.*] Now are
                they come. [*Exit Provost.*   80
This is a gentle provost; seldom when
The steelèd gaoler is the friend of men.

    Enter the PROVOST, *as knocking resumes.*

How now, what noise! That spirit's possessed with haste
That wounds th'unshifting postern with these strokes.
PROVOST There he must stay until the officer
Arise to let him in: he is called up.[104]
DUKE   Have you no countermand for Claudio yet,
But he must die tomorrow?
PROVOST   None, sir, none.
DUKE   As near the dawning, Provost, as it is,
You shall hear more ere morning.
PROVOST   Happily   90
You something know; yet I believe there comes
No countermand; no such example have we.

Besides, upon the very siege of justice,
Lord Angelo hath to the public ear
Professed the contrary.

Enter a MESSENGER.

　　　　　　　　　　　This is his lordship's man.[105]

DUKE　　　And here comes Claudio's pardon.

MESSEN.　[*giving Provost a paper:*] My lord hath sent you this note;
and by me this further charge, that you swerve not from
the smallest article of it, neither in time, matter, or
other circumstance. Good morrow; for as I take it, it is　100
almost day.

PROVOST　I shall obey him.　　　　　　　　　　　[*Exit messenger.*

DUKE　　　[*aside:*] This is his pardon, purchased by such sin
For which the pardoner himself is in.
Hence hath offence his quick celerity,
When it is borne in high authority.
When vice makes mercy, mercy's so extended
That for the fault's love is th'offender friended.
– Now, sir, what news?

PROVOST　I told you: Lord Angelo, belike thinking me remiss in　110
mine office, awakens me with this unwonted putting-
on; methinks strangely, for he hath not used it before.

DUKE　　　Pray you, let's hear.

PROVOST　[*reads:*] 'Whatsoever you may hear to the contrary, let
Claudio be executed by four of the clock, and, in the
afternoon, Barnardine. For my better satisfaction, let me
have Claudio's head sent me by five. Let this be duly
performed, with a thought that more depends on it
than we must yet deliver. Thus fail not to do your
office, as you will answer it at your peril.' – What say　120
you to this, sir?

DUKE　　　What is that Barnardine who is to be executed in th'
afternoon?

PROVOST　A Bohemian born; but here nursed up and bred.
One that is a prisoner nine years old.

DUKE　　　How came it that the absent Duke had not either
delivered him to his liberty or executed him? I have
heard it was ever his manner to do so.

PROVOST   His friends still wrought reprieves for him; and indeed, his fact, till now in the government of Lord Angelo, 130 came not to an undoubtful proof.

DUKE   It is now apparent?

PROVOST   Most manifest, and not denied by himself.

DUKE   Hath he borne himself penitently in prison? How seems he to be touched?

PROVOST   A man that apprehends death no more dreadfully but as a drunken sleep; careless, reckless, and fearless, of what's past, present, or to come; insensible of mortality, and desperately mortal.[106]

DUKE   He wants advice.   140

PROVOST   He will hear none. He hath evermore had the liberty of the prison; give him leave to escape hence, he would not. Drunk many times a day, if not many days entirely drunk. We have very oft awaked him, as if to carry him to execution, and showed him a seeming warrant for it; it hath not moved him at all.

DUKE   More of him anon. There is written in your brow, Provost, honesty and constancy: if I read it not truly, my ancient skill beguiles me; but in the boldness of my cunning, I will lay myself in hazard. Claudio, whom 150 here you have warrant to execute, is no greater forfeit to the law than Angelo who hath sentenced him. To make you understand this in a manifested effect, I crave but four days' respite; for the which you are to do me both a present and a dangerous courtesy.

PROVOST   Pray sir, in what?

DUKE   In the delaying death.

PROVOST   Alack! How may I do it, having the hour limited, and an express command, under penalty, to deliver his head in the view of Angelo? I may make my case as 160 Claudio's, to cross this in the smallest.

DUKE   By the vow of mine Order, I warrant you, if my instructions may be your guide. Let this Barnardine be this morning executed, and his head borne to Angelo.

PROVOST   Angelo hath seen them both, and will discover the favour.

DUKE   O, death's a great disguiser; and you may add to it.

Shave the head and tie the beard, and say it was the desire of the penitent to be so bared before his death: you know the course is common. If anything fall to you upon this more than thanks and good fortune, by the saint whom I profess, I will plead against it with my life. 170

PROVOST   Pardon me, good father; it is against my oath.

DUKE   Were you sworn to the Duke, or to the deputy?

PROVOST   To him and to his substitutes.

DUKE   You will think you have made no offence, if the Duke avouch the justice of your dealing?

PROVOST   But what likelihood is in that?

DUKE   Not a resemblance, but a certainty. Yet since I see you fearful, that neither my coat, integrity, nor persuasion, 180 can with ease attempt you, I will go further than I meant, to pluck all fears out of you. [*He produces a letter.*] Look you, sir, here is the hand and seal of the Duke. You know the character, I doubt not; and the signet is not strange to you.

PROVOST   I know them both.

DUKE   The contents of this is the return of the Duke; you shall anon over-read it at your pleasure, where you shall find within these two days he will be here. This is a thing that Angelo knows not; for he this very day receives 190 letters of strange tenor, perchance of the Duke's death, perchance entering into some monastery; but, by chance, nothing of what is writ. – Look, th'unfolding star calls up the shepherd. – Put not yourself into amazement how these things should be; all difficulties are but easy when they are known. Call your executioner, and off with Barnardine's head. I will give him a present shrift, and advise him for a better place. Yet you are amazed, but this shall absolutely resolve you. Come away; it is almost clear dawn.   [*Exeunt.* 200

SCENE 3.

Inside the prison.

Enter POMPEY.

POMPEY   I am as well acquainted here as I was in our house of profession: one would think it were Mistress Overdone's own house, for here be many of her old customers. First, here's young Master Rash: he's in for a commodity of brown paper and old ginger, nine score and seventeen pounds, of which he made five marks ready money. Marry, then ginger was not much in request, for the old women were all dead.[107] Then is there here one Master Caper, at the suit of Master Three-Pile the mercer, for some four suits of peach-coloured satin, which now   10 peaches him a beggar. Then have we here young Dizzy, and young Master Deep-Vow, and Master Copper-Spur, and Master Starve-Lackey, the rapier and dagger man, and young Drop-Heir that killed lusty Pudding, and Master Forthright the tilter, and brave Master Shoe-Tie the great traveller, and wild Half-Can that stabbed Pots, and, I think, forty more, all great doers in our trade, and are now 'for the Lord's sake'.[108]

Enter ABHORSON.

ABHOR.   Sirrah, bring Barnardine hither.

POMPEY   Master Barnardine! You must rise and be hanged, Master   20 Barnardine!

ABHOR.   What ho, Barnardine!

BARNARD.   [*within:*] A pox o'your throats! Who makes that noise there? What are you?

POMPEY   Your friends, sir; the hangman. You must be so good, sir, to rise and be put to death.

BARNARD.   [*within:*] Away, you rogue, away; I am sleepy.

ABHOR.   Tell him he must awake, and that quickly too.

POMPEY   Pray, Master Barnardine, awake till you are executed, and sleep afterwards.   30

ABHOR.   Go in to him, and fetch him out.

POMPEY   He is coming, sir, he is coming; I hear his straw rustle.

Enter BARNARDINE.

ABHOR.   [*to Pompey:*] Is the axe upon the block, sirrah?

POMPEY   Very ready, sir.

BARNARD. How now, Abhorson, what's the news with you?

ABHOR.   Truly, sir, I would desire you to clap into your prayers; for, look you, the warrant's come.

BARNARD. You rogue, I have been drinking all night; I am not fitted for't.

POMPEY   O, the better, sir: for he that drinks all night, and is   40
          hanged betimes in the morning, may sleep the sounder all the next day.

Enter the DUKE *(disguised as friar).*

ABHOR.   [*to Barnardine:*] Look you, sir, here comes your ghostly father. Do we jest now, think you?

DUKE   [*to Barnardine:*] Sir, induced by my charity, and hearing how hastily you are to depart, I am come to advise you, comfort you, and pray with you.

BARNARD. Friar, not I; I have been drinking hard all night, and I will have more time to prepare me, or they shall beat out my brains with billets. I will not consent to die this   50
          day, that's certain.

DUKE   O, sir, you must; and therefore, I beseech you,
          Look forward on the journey you shall go.

BARNARD. I swear I will not die today for any man's persuasion.

DUKE   But hear you —

BARNARD. Not a word; if you have anything to say to me, come to my ward; for thence will not I today.   [*Exit.*

Enter the PROVOST.

DUKE   Unfit to live or die; O gravel heart!
          — After him, fellows; bring him to the block.[109]
                              [*Exeunt Abhorson and Pompey.*

PROVOST   Now, sir, how do you find the prisoner?   60

DUKE   A creature unprepared, unmeet for death;
          And to transport him in the mind he is
          Were damnable.

PROVOST   Here in the prison, father,
          There died this morning of a cruel fever

   One Ragozine, a most notorious pirate,
   A man of Claudio's years; his beard and head
   Just of his colour. What if we do omit
   This reprobate till he were well inclined,
   And satisfy the deputy with the visage
   Of Ragozine, more like to Claudio?   70
DUKE O, 'tis an accident that Heaven provides!
   Dispatch it presently; the hour draws on
   Prefixed by Angelo. See this be done,
   And sent according to command; whiles I
   Persuade this rude wretch willingly to die.
PROVOST This shall be done, good father, presently.
   But Barnardine must die this afternoon;
   And how shall we continue Claudio,
   To save me from the danger that might come
   If he were known alive?
DUKE   Let this be done: 80
   Put them in secret holds, both Barnardine and Claudio.
   Ere twice the sun hath made his journal greeting
   To yonder generation,[110] you shall find
   Your safety manifested.
PROVOST I am your free dependant.
DUKE Quick, dispatch, and send the head to Angelo.
             [*Exit Provost.*
   Now will I write letters to Varrius – [111]
   The Provost, he shall bear them – whose conténts
   Shall witness to him I am near at home,
   And that, by great injunctions, I am bound   90
   To enter publicly. Him I'll desire
   To meet me at the consecrated fount,
   A league below the city; and from thence,
   By cold gradation and well-balanced form.
   We shall proceed with Angelo.

    Enter the PROVOST, *carrying a box.*[112]

PROVOST Here is the head; I'll carry it myself.
DUKE Convenient is it. Make a swift return,
   For I would cómmune with you of such things
   That want no ear but yours.
PROVOST   I'll make all speed. [*Exit.*

ISABELLA	[*beyond:*] Peace, ho, be here!	100
DUKE	The tongue of Isabel. She's come to know	
	If yet her brother's pardon be come hither;	
	But I will keep her ignorant of her good,	
	To make her heavenly comforts of despair	
	When it is least expected.	

Enter ISABELLA.

ISABELLA	Ho, by your leave!	
DUKE	Good morning to you, fair and gracious daughter.	
ISABELLA	The better, given me by so holy a man.	
	Hath yet the deputy sent my brother's pardon?	
DUKE	He hath released him, Isabel, from the world.	
	His head is off, and sent to Angelo.	110
ISABELLA	Nay, but it is not so.	
DUKE	It is no other.	
	Show your wisdom, daughter, in your close patience.	
ISABELLA	O, I will to him and pluck out his eyes!	
DUKE	You shall not be admitted to his sight.	
ISABELLA	Unhappy Claudio, wretched Isabel,	
	Injurious world! Most damnèd Angelo!	
DUKE	This nor hurts him, nor profits you a jot;	
	Forbear it, therefore; give your cause to Heaven.	
	Mark what I say, which you shall find	
	By every syllable a faithful verity.	120
	The Duke comes home tomorrow. Nay, dry your eyes.	
	One of our covent, and his cónfessor,[113]	
	Gives me this instance: already he hath carried	
	Notice to Escalus and Angelo,	
	Who do prepare to meet him at the gates,	
	There to give up their pow'r. If you can, pace	
	your wisdom	
	In that good path that I would wish it go,	
	And you shall have your bosom on this wretch,	
	Grace of the Duke, revenges to your heart,	
	And general honour.	
ISABELLA	I am directed by you.	130
DUKE	[*producing a letter:*] This letter, then, to Friar Peter give;	
	'Tis that he sent me of the Duke's return.	
	Say, by this token, I desire his company	

At Mariana's house tonight. Her cause and yours
I'll pérfect him withal; and he shall bring you
Before the Duke; and to the head of Angelo
Accuse him home and home. For my poor self,
I am combinèd by a sacred vow,
And shall be absent. Wend you with this letter.
Command these fretting waters from your eyes   140
With a light heart; trust not my holy Order,
If I pervert your course. – Who's here?

            Enter LUCIO.

LUCIO   Good even. Friar, where's the Provost?
DUKE   Not within, sir.
LUCIO   O pretty Isabella, I am pale at mine heart to see thine
eyes so red: thou must be patient. I am fain to dine and
sup with water and bran: I dare not, for my head, fill my
belly: one fruitful meal would set me to't.[114] But they say
the Duke will be here tomorrow. By my troth, Isabel,
I loved thy brother. If the old fantastical Duke of Dark   150
Corners had been at home, he had lived.[115] [*Exit Isabella.*
DUKE   Sir, the Duke is marvellous little beholding to your
reports; but the best is, he lives not in them.
LUCIO   Friar, thou knowest not the Duke so well as I do; he's
a better woodman than thou tak'st him for.
DUKE   Well, you'll answer this one day. Fare ye well.
LUCIO   Nay, tarry; I'll go along with thee; I can tell thee
pretty tales of the Duke.
DUKE   You have told me too many of him already, sir, if they
be true; if not true, none were enough.   160
LUCIO   I was once before him for getting a wench with child.
DUKE   Did you such a thing?
LUCIO   Yes, marry, did I; but I was fain to forswear it: they
would else have married me to the rotten medlar.
DUKE   Sir, your company is fairer than honest. Rest you well.
LUCIO   By my troth, I'll go with thee to the lane's end. If
bawdy talk offend you, we'll have very little of it. Nay,
friar, I am a kind of burr; I shall stick.   [*Exeunt.*

SCENE 4.

Inside ANGELO'S *house.*

Enter ANGELO *and* ESCALUS.

ESCALUS   Every letter he hath writ hath disvouched other.

ANGELO   In most uneven and distracted manner. His actions
show much like to madness; pray Heaven his wisdom
be not tainted! And why meet him at the gates, and
re-deliver our authorities there?[116]

ESCALUS   I guess not.

ANGELO   And why should we proclaim it, in an hour before his
entering, that if any crave redress of injustice, they
should exhibit their petitions in the street?

ESCALUS   He shows his reason for that: to have a dispatch of   10
complaints; and to deliver us from devices hereafter,
which shall then have no power to stand against us.

ANGELO   Well; I beseech you, let it be proclaimed betimes i'th'
morn. I'll call you at your house. Give notice to such
men of sort and suit as are to meet him.[117]

ESCALUS   I shall, sir; fare you well.

ANGELO   Good night.   [*Exit Escalus.*
          This deed unshapes me quite, makes me unpregnant
          And dull to all proceedings. A deflow'red maid,
          And by an eminent body that enforced   20
          The law against it! But that her tender shame
          Will not proclaim against her maiden loss,
          How might she tongue me? Yet reason dares her no;
          For my authority bears a so credent bulk[118]
          That no particular scandal once can touch,
          But it confounds the breather. He should have lived,
          Save that his riotous youth, with dangerous sense,
          Might in the times to come have ta'en revenge,[119]
          By so receiving a dishonoured life
          With ransom of such shame. Would yet he had lived!   30
          Alack, when once our grace we have forgot,
          Nothing goes right; we would, and we would not.
                                             [*Exit.*

SCENE 5.

Outside the city.[120]

Enter the DUKE *(not disguised) and* FRIAR PETER.

DUKE   [*giving letters:*] These letters at fit time deliver me.
          The Provost knows our purpose and our plot.
          The matter being afoot, keep your instruction
          And hold you ever to our special drift;
          Though sometimes you do blench from this to that
          As cause doth minister. Go, call at Flavius' house,[121]
          And tell him where I stay; give the like notice
          To Valentinus, Rowland, and to Crassus,
          And bid them bring the trumpets to the gate;
          But send me Flavius first.   10
PETER   It shall be speeded well.   [*Exit Friar.*

              Enter VARRIUS.

DUKE   I thank thee, Varrius; thou hast made good haste.
          Come, we will walk. There's other of our friends
          Will greet us here anon. My gentle Varrius!   [*Exeunt.*

SCENE 6.

A street near the city gates.

Enter ISABELLA *and* MARIANA.

ISABELLA   To speak so indirectly I am loath;
           I would say the truth; but to accuse him so,
           That is your part. Yet I am advised to do it;
           He says, to veil full purpose.

MARIANA   Be ruled by him.

ISABELLA   Besides, he tells me that, if peradventure
           He speak against me on the adverse side,
           I should not think it strange; for 'tis a physic
           That's bitter to sweet end.

MARIANA   I would Friar Peter –

Enter FRIAR PETER.

ISABELLA   O peace! The friar is come.

PETER   Come, I have found you out a stand most fit,   10
           Where you may have such vantage on the Duke,
           He shall not pass you. Twice have the trumpets
                                                    sounded.
           The generous and gravest citizens
           Have hent the gates, and very near upon
           The Duke is ent'ring; therefore hence, away. [*Exeunt.*

ACT 5, SCENE I.

The city gates.

Enter, at one door, the DUKE, VARRIUS *and* LORDS; *at another,*
ANGELO *and* ESCALUS, *followed by* LUCIO, OFFICERS *and* CITIZENS.

DUKE	My very worthy cousin, fairly met!
	Our old and faithful friend, we are glad to see you.
ANG., ESC.	Happy return be to your royal Grace!
DUKE	Many and hearty thankings to you both.
	We have made inquiry of you, and we hear
	Such goodness of your justice that our soul
	Cannot but yield you forth to public thanks,
	Fore-running more requital.
ANGELO	You make my bonds still greater.
DUKE	O, your desert speaks loud; and I should wrong it 10
	To lock it in the wards of covert bosom,
	When it deserves, with characters of brass,
	A forted residence 'gainst the tooth of time
	And razure of oblivion. Give me your hand,
	And let the subject see, to make them know
	That outward courtesies would fain proclaim
	Favours that keep within. Come, Escalus,
	You must walk by us on our other hand,
	And good supporters are you.

Enter FRIAR PETER *and* ISABELLA.

PETER	Now is your time; speak loud, and kneel before him. 20
ISABELLA	Justice, O royal Duke! [*She kneels.*] Vail your regard
	Upon a wronged – I would fain have said, 'a maid'.
	O worthy Prince, dishonour not your eye
	By throwing it on any other object
	Till you have heard me in my true complaint,
	And given me justice, justice, justice, justice!
DUKE	Relate your wrongs: in what? By whom? Be brief.
	Here is Lord Angelo shall give you justice;
	Reveal yourself to him.
ISABELLA	O worthy Duke,

You bid me seek redemption of the Devil!
Hear me yourself; for that which I must speak
Must either punish me, not being believed,
Or wring redress from you. Hear me, O hear me, here!

ANGELO My lord, her wits, I fear me, are not firm;
She hath been a suitor to me for her brother,
Cut off by course of justice –

ISABELLA [*standing:*] 'By course of justice'!

ANGELO And she will speak most bitterly and strange.

ISABELLA Most strange, but yet most truly, will I speak.
That Angelo's forsworn, is it not strange?
That Angelo's a murtherer, is't not strange?
That Angelo is an adulterous thief,
An hypocrite, a virgin-violator,
Is it not strange and strange?

DUKE Nay, it is ten times strange!

ISABELLA It is not truer he is Angelo
Than this is all as true as it is strange;
Nay, it is ten times true, for truth is truth
To th'end of reck'ning.[122]

DUKE Away with her. Poor soul,
She speaks this in th'infirmity of sense.

ISABELLA O Prince! I conjure thee, as thou believ'st
There is another comfort than this world,
That thou neglect me not with that opinion
That I am touched with madness. Make not impossible
That which but seems unlike: 'tis not impossible
But one, the wicked'st caitiff on the ground,
May seem as shy, as grave, as just, as absolute,
As Angelo; even so may Angelo,
In all his dressings, caracts, titles, forms,
Be an arch-villain. Believe it, royal Prince,
If he be less, he's nothing; but he's more,
Had I more name for badness.

DUKE By mine honesty,
If she be mad, as I believe no other,
Her madness hath the oddest frame of sense,
Such a dependency of thing on thing,
As e'er I heard in madness.

ISABELLA   O gracious Duke,
Harp not on that; nor do not banish reason
For inequality;[123] but let your reason serve
To make the truth appear where it seems hid,
And hide the false seems true.

DUKE   Many that are not mad   70
Have, sure, more lack of reason. What would you say?

ISABELLA   I am the sister of one Claudio,
Condemned upon the act of fornication
To lose his head; condemned by Angelo.
I (in probation of a sisterhood)
Was sent to by my brother; one Lucio
As then the messenger –

LUCIO   That's I, and't like your Grace:
I came to her from Claudio, and desired her
To try her gracious fortune with Lord Angelo   80
For her poor brother's pardon.

ISABELLA   That's he indeed.

DUKE   [*to Lucio:*] You were not bid to speak.

LUCIO   No, my good lord;
Nor wished to hold my peace.

DUKE   I wish you now, then;
Pray you take note of it; and when you have
A business for yourself, pray Heaven you then
Be perfect.

LUCIO   I warrant your Honour.

DUKE   The warrant's for yourself; take heed to't.

ISABELLA   This gentleman told somewhat of my tale.

LUCIO   Right.

DUKE   It may be right; but you are i'the wrong   90
To speak before your time. – Proceed.

ISABELLA   I went
To this pernicious caitiff deputy –

DUKE   That's somewhat madly spoken.

ISABELLA   Pardon it;
The phrase is to the matter.

DUKE   Mended again.
The matter: proceed.

ISABELLA   In brief, to set the needless process by:

How I persuaded, how I prayed, and kneeled,
How he refelled me, and how I replied
(For this was of much length); the vile conclusion
I now begin with grief and shame to utter: 100
He would not, but by gift of my chaste body
To his concupiscible intemperate lust,
Release my brother; and, after much debatement,
My sisterly remorse confutes mine honour,
And I did yield to him. But the next morn betimes,
His purpose surfeiting, he sends a warrant
For my poor brother's head.

DUKE   This is most likely!

ISABELLA   O that it were as like as it is true!

DUKE   By Heaven, fond wretch, thou know'st not what thou
                                                speak'st,
            Or else thou art suborned against his honour   110
            In hateful practice. First, his integrity
            Stands without blemish; next, it imports no reason
            That with such vehemency he should pursue
            Faults proper to himself. If he had so offended,
            He would have weighed thy brother by himself,
            And not have cut him off. Some one hath set you on:
            Confess the truth, and say by whose advice
            Thou cam'st here to complain.

ISABELLA   And is this all?
            Then O, you blessèd ministers above,
            Keep me in patience, and, with ripened time,   120
            Unfold the evil which is here wrapped up
            In countenance! Heaven shield your Grace from woe,
            As I, thus wronged, hence unbelievèd go!

DUKE   I know you'd fain be gone. – An officer!
            To prison with her! – Shall we thus permit
            A blasting and a scandalous breath to fall
            On him so near us? This needs must be a practice.

                                    [*An officer arrests Isabella.*
            – Who knew of your intent and coming hither?

ISABELLA   One that I would were here, Friar Lodowick.

DUKE   A ghostly father, belike. – Who knows that Lodowick? 130

LUCIO   My lord, I know him; 'tis a meddling friar.

	I do not like the man; had he been lay, my lord,
	For certain words he spake against your Grace
	In your retirement, I had swinged him soundly.
DUKE	Words against me? This' a good friar, belike!
	And to set on this wretched woman here
	Against our substitute! Let this friar be found.
LUCIO	But yesternight, my lord, she and that friar,
	I saw them at the prison; a saucy friar,
	A very scurvy fellow.

PETER Blessed be your royal Grace!
     I have stood by, my lord, and I have heard
     Your royal ear abused. First hath this woman
     Most wrongfully accused your substitute,
     Who is as free from touch or soil with her
     As she from one ungot.
DUKE We did believe no less.
     Know you that Friar Lodowick that she speaks of?
PETER I know him for a man divine and holy;
     Not scurvy, nor a temporary meddler,
     As he's reported by this gentleman;
     And, on my trust, a man that never yet
     Did (as he vouches) misreport your Grace.
LUCIO My lord, most villainously; believe it.
PETER Well, he in time may come to clear himself;
     But at this instant he is sick, my lord,
     Of a strange fever. Upon his mere request,
     Being come to knowledge that there was complaint
     Intended 'gainst Lord Angelo, came I hither
     To speak, as from his mouth, what he doth know
     Is true and false; and what he, with his oath
     And all probation, will make up full clear,
     Whensoever he's convénted. First, for this woman:
     To justify this worthy nobleman,
     So vulgarly and personally accused,
     Her shall you hear disprovèd to her eyes,
     Till she herself confess it.
DUKE   Good friar, let's hear it.
     – Do you not smile at this, Lord Angelo?
     O Heaven, the vanity of wretched fools! –

140

150

160

	Give us some seats. [*Two seats are provided.*

Give us some seats.   [*Two seats are provided.*
                        Come, cousin Angelo;   170
In this I'll be impartial: be you judge
Of your own cause. [*Both sit. Exeunt officer and Isabella.*

   Enter MARIANA, *veiled, led by* FRIAR PETER.

             – Is this the witness, friar?
First let her show her face, and after speak.

MARIANA   Pardon, my lord; I will not show my face
Until my husband bid me.

DUKE   What, are you married?

MARIANA   No, my lord.

DUKE   Are you a maid?

MARIANA   No, my lord.

DUKE   A widow, then?

MARIANA   Neither, my lord.   180

DUKE   Why, you are nothing then; neither maid, widow, nor wife.

LUCIO   My lord, she may be a punk; for many of them are neither maid, widow, nor wife.

DUKE   Silence that fellow. I would he had some cause to prattle for himself.[124]

LUCIO   Well, my lord.

MARIANA   My lord, I do confess I ne'er was married,
And I confess, besides, I am no maid.
I have known my husband; yet my husband   190
Knows not that ever he knew me.[125]

LUCIO   He was drunk, then, my lord; it can be no better.

DUKE   For the benefit of silence, would thou wert so too!

LUCIO   Well, my lord.

DUKE   This is no witness for Lord Angelo.

MARIANA   Now I come to't, my lord:
She that accuses him of fornication,
In self-same manner doth accuse my husband;
And charges him, my lord, with such a time
When I'll depose I had him in mine arms,   200
With all th'effect of love.

ANGELO   Charges she moe than me?

MARIANA   Not that I know.

DUKE   No? You say your husband.

MARIANA   Why, just, my lord, and that is Angelo,
           Who thinks he knows that he ne'er knew my body,
           But knows, he thinks, that he knows Isabel's.

ANGELO   This is a strange abuse. Let's see thy face.

MARIANA   My husband bids me; now I will unmask.

                                    [*She unveils her face.*

           This is that face, thou cruel Angelo,
           Which once thou swor'st was worth the looking on;   210
           This is the hand which, with a vowed contráct,
           Was fast belocked in thine; this is the body
           That took away the match from Isabel,
           And did supply thee at thy garden-house
           In her imagined person.

DUKE   [*to Angelo:*]   Know you this woman?

LUCIO   Carnally, she says.

DUKE   Sirrah, no more!

LUCIO   Enough, my lord.

ANGELO   My lord, I must confess I know this woman;
           And, five years since, there was some speech of marriage 220
           Betwixt myself and her; which was broke off,
           Partly for that her promised proportions
           Came short of composition; but in chief
           For that her reputation was disvalued
           In levity. Since which time of five years,
           I never spake with her, saw her, nor heard from her,
           Upon my faith and honour.

MARIANA   [*kneeling:*]   Noble Prince,
           As there comes light from Heaven and words from
                                                       breath,
           As there is sense in truth, and truth in virtue,
           I am affianced this man's wife, as strongly   230
           As words could make up vows. And, my good lord,
           But Tuesday night last gone, in's garden-house,
           He knew me as a wife. As this is true,
           Let me in safety raise me from my knees,
           .Or else for ever be confixèd here,
           A marble monument.

ANGELO   I did but smile till now.

	Now, good my lord, give me the scope of justice;

Now, good my lord, give me the scope of justice;
My patience here is touched. I do perceive
These poor informal women are no more   240
But instruments of some more mightier member
That sets them on. Let me have way, my lord,
To find this practice out.

DUKE   [*standing:*]   Ay, with my heart;
And punish them to your height of pleasure.
– Thou foolish friar, and thou pernicious woman,
Compáct with her that's gone, think'st thou thy oaths,
Though they would swear down each particular saint,
Were testimonies against his worth and credit,
That's sealed in approbation? – You, Lord Escalus,
Sit with my cousin; lend him your kind pains   250
To find out this abuse, whence 'tis derived.
There is another friar that set them on;
Let him be sent for.

PETER   Would he were here, my lord, for he indeed
Hath set the women on to this complaint.
Your provost knows the place where he abides,
And he may fetch him.

DUKE   Go, do it instantly. [*Exit Provost.*
And you, my noble and well-warranted cousin,
Whom it concerns to hear this matter forth,
Do with your injuries as seems you best   260
In any chástisement. I for a while will leave you;
But stir not you till you have well determined
Upon these slanderers.

ESCALUS   My lord, we'll do it throughly.
                                    [*Exit Duke.*
Signor Lucio, did not you say you knew that Friar
Lodowick to be a dishonest person?

LUCIO   'Cucullus non facit monachum': honest in nothing but in
his clothes; and one that hath spoke most villainous
speeches of the Duke.

ESCALUS   We shall entreat you to abide here till he come, and
enforce them against him. We shall find this friar a   270
notable fellow.

LUCIO   As any in Vienna, on my word.

ESCALUS   Call that same Isabel here once again; I would speak
           with her.   [*Exit an attendant.*
           [*To Angelo:*] Pray you, my lord, give me leave to question;
           you shall see how I'll handle her.

LUCIO   Not better than he, by her own report.

ESCALUS   Say you?

LUCIO   Marry, sir, I think, if you handled her privately, she
          would sooner confess; perchance, publicly, she'll be   280
          ashamed.

                 Enter an OFFICER *with* ISABELLA.

ESCALUS   I will go darkly to work with her.

LUCIO   That's the way, for women are light at midnight.

ESCALUS   Come on, mistress; here's a gentlewoman denies all
           that you have said.

       Enter the DUKE (*disguised as friar*) *with the* PROVOST.

LUCIO   My lord, here comes the rascal I spoke of, here with
          the Provost.

ESCALUS   In very good time. Speak not you to him till we call
           upon you.

LUCIO   Mum.   290

ESCALUS   [*to the Duke:*] Come, sir; did you set these women on
           to slander Lord Angelo? They have confessed you did.

DUKE   'Tis false.

ESCALUS   How? Know you where you are?

DUKE   Respect your great place; and let the Devil
          Be sometime honoured for his burning throne.[126]
          Where is the Duke? 'Tis he should hear me speak.

ESCALUS   The Duke's in us, and we will hear you speak.
           Look you speak justly.

DUKE   Boldly, at least. But O, poor souls,
          Come you to seek the lamb here of the fox?   300
          Good night to your redress! Is the Duke gone?
          Then is your cause gone too. The Duke's unjust,
          Thus to retort your manifest appeal,
          And put your trial in the villain's mouth
          Which here you come to accuse.

LUCIO   This is the rascal: this is he I spoke of.

ESCALUS   Why, thou unreverend and unhallowed friar,

Is't not enough thou hast suborned these women
To accuse this worthy man, but, in foul mouth,
And in the witness of his proper ear,   310
To call him 'villain'; and then to glance from him
To th'Duke himself, to tax him with injustice?
– Take him hence; to th'rack with him! – We'll
                                        towze you
Joint by joint – but we will know his purpose.
What, 'unjust'?

DUKE   Be not so hot; the Duke
Dare no more stretch this finger of mine than he
Dare rack his own; his subject am I not,
Nor here provincial.[127] My business in this state
Made me a looker-on here in Vienna,
Where I have seen corruption boil and bubble   320
Till it o'er-run the stew: laws for all faults,
But faults so countenanced that the strong statutes
Stand like the forfeits in a barber's shop,
As much in mock as mark.[128]

ESCALUS   Slander to th'state!
Away with him to prison!

ANGELO   What can you vouch against him, Signor Lucio?
Is this the man that you did tell us of?

LUCIO   'Tis he, my lord. – Come hither, Goodman Bald-Pate.
Do you know me?

DUKE   I remember you, sir, by the sound of your voice. I met   330
you at the prison, in the absence of the Duke.

LUCIO   O, did you so? And do you remember what you said
of the Duke?

DUKE   Most notedly, sir.

LUCIO   Do you so, sir? And was the Duke a fleshmonger, a
fool, and a coward, as you then reported him to be?

DUKE   You must, sir, change persons with me, ere you make
that my report. You, indeed, spoke so of him, and
much more, much worse.

LUCIO   O thou damnable fellow! Did not I pluck thee by the   340
nose for thy speeches?

DUKE   I protest, I love the Duke as I love myself.

ANGELO   Hark how the villain would close now, after his

treasonable abuses!

ESCALUS   Such a fellow is not to be talked withal. Away with him to prison! Where is the Provost? Away with him to prison! Lay bolts enough upon him; let him speak no more. Away with those giglets too, and with the other confederate companion!

     [*Mariana is seized. The Provost lays hands on the Duke.*

DUKE   Stay, sir; stay a while.   350

ANGELO   What, resists he? – Help him, Lucio.

LUCIO   Come sir, come sir, come sir! Foh, sir! Why, you bald-pated lying rascal, you must be hooded, must you? Show your knave's visage, with a pox to you! Show your sheep-biting face, and be hanged an hour! Will't not off?

     [*He pulls off the friar's hood and reveals the Duke.*

DUKE   Thou art the first knave that e'er mad'st a duke.
– First, Provost, let me bail these gentle three.
[*To Lucio:*] Sneak not away, sir, for the friar and you
Must have a word anon. – Lay hold on him.   360

     [*Lucio is seized.*

LUCIO   [*aside:*] This may prove worse than hanging.

DUKE   [*to Escalus:*] What you have spoke, I pardon; sit you
                             down.
We'll borrow place of him. [*To Angelo:*] Sir, by your
                             leave.

     [*He takes Angelo's place.*

Hast thou or word, or wit, or impudence,
That yet can do thee office? If thou hast,
Rely upon it till my tale be heard,
And hold no longer out.

ANGELO   O, my dread lord,
I should be guiltier than my guiltiness,
To think I can be undiscernible,
When I perceive your Grace, like pow'r divine,   370
Hath looked upon my passes. Then, good Prince,
No longer session hold upon my shame,
But let my trial be mine own confession.
Immediate sentence then, and sequent death,
Is all the grace I beg.

DUKE   Come hither, Mariana.
           [*To Angelo:*] Say, wast thou e'er contracted to this woman?
ANGELO   I was, my lord.
DUKE   Go, take her hence, and marry her instantly.
           – Do you the office, friar; which consummate,   380
           Return him here again. – Go with him, Provost.
                     [*Exeunt Angelo, Mariana, Friar Peter and Provost.*
ESCALUS   My lord, I am more amazed at his dishonour
           Than at the strangeness of it.
DUKE   Come hither, Isabel.
           Your friar is now your prince. As I was then,
           Advértising and holy to your business,
           Not changing heart with habit, I am still
           Attorneyed at your service.
ISABELLA   O, give me pardon,
           That I, your vassal, have employed and pained
           Your unknown sovereignty.   390
DUKE   You are pardoned, Isabel.
           And now, dear maid, be you as free to us.
           Your brother's death, I know, sits at your heart;
           And you may marvel why I obscured myself,
           Labouring to save his life, and would not rather
           Make rash remonstrance of my hidden pow'r
           Than let him so be lost. O most kind maid,
           It was the swift celerity of his death,
           Which I did think with slower foot came on,
           That brained my purpose. But peace be with him!   400
           That life is better life, past fearing death,
           Than that which lives to fear. Make it your comfort,
           So happy is your brother.
ISABELLA   I do, my lord.

           Enter ANGELO, MARIANA, FRIAR PETER *and the* PROVOST.

DUKE   For this new-married man approaching here,
           Whose salt imagination yet hath wronged
           Your well-defended honour, you must pardon
           For Mariana's sake; but as he adjudged your brother,
           Being criminal in double violation
           Of sacred chastity and of promise-breach,
           Thereon dependent, for your brother's life,[129]   410

The very mercy of the law cries out
Most audible, even from his proper tongue,
'An Angelo for Claudio, death for death!
Haste still pays haste, and leisure answers leisure;
Like doth quit like, and measure still for measure!'[130]
Then, Angelo, thy fault's thus manifested,
Which, though thou wouldst deny, denies

                              thee vantage.
We do condemn thee to the very block
Where Claudio stooped to death, and with like haste.
– Away with him!

MARIANA   O my most gracious lord,   420
I hope you will not mock me with a husband!

DUKE   It is your husband mocked you with a husband.
Consenting to the safeguard of your honour,
I thought your marriage fit; else imputation,
For that he knew you, might reproach your life,
And choke your good to come. For his possessions,
Although by confiscation they are ours,
We do instate and widow you with all,
To buy you a better husband.

MARIANA   O my dear lord,
I crave no other, nor no better man.   430

DUKE   Never crave him; we are definitive.

MARIANA [kneeling:] Gentle my liege –

DUKE   You do but lose your labour.
Away with him to death! [To Lucio:] Now, sir, to you.

MARIANA O my good lord! – Sweet Isabel, take my part:
Lend me your knees, and all my life to come
I'll lend you all my life to do you service.

DUKE   Against all sense you do impórtune her.
Should she kneel down in mercy of this fact,
Her brother's ghost his pavèd bed would break,
And take her hence in horror.

MARIANA   Isabel,   440
Sweet Isabel, do yet but kneel by me;
Hold up your hands, say nothing; I'll speak all.
They say best men are moulded out of faults,
And, for the most, become much more the better

	For being a little bad; so may my husband.
	O Isabel, will you not lend a knee?
DUKE	He dies for Claudio's death.
ISABELLA	[*kneeling:*] Most bounteous sir,

Look, if it please you, on this man condemned,
As if my brother lived. I partly think
A due sincerity governed his deeds   450
Till he did look on me. Since it is so,
Let him not die. My brother had but justice,
In that he did the thing for which he died.
For Angelo,
His act did not o'ertake his bad intent,
And must be buried but as an intent
That perished by the way. Thoughts are no subjects;
Intents but merely thoughts.[131]

MARIANA	Merely, my lord.
DUKE	Your suit's unprofitable; stand up, I say.

                                  [*Mariana and Isabella stand.*

I have bethought me of another fault.   460
 – Provost, how came it Claudio was beheaded
At an unusual hour?

PROVOST	It was commanded so.
DUKE	Had you a special warrant for the deed?
PROVOST	No, my good lord; it was by private message.
DUKE	For which I do discharge you of your office:
	Give up your keys.
PROVOST	Pardon me, noble lord;

I thought it was a fault, but knew it not;
Yet did repent me, after more advice;
For testimony whereof, one in the prison,   470
That should by private order else have died,
I have reserved alive.

DUKE	What's he?
PROVOST	His name is Barnardine.
DUKE	I would thou hadst done so by Claudio.
	Go fetch him hither; let me look upon him.

                                    [*Exit Provost.*

ESCALUS	I am sorry one so learnèd and so wise
	As you, Lord Angelo, have still appeared,

	Should slip so grossly, both in the heat of blood
	And lack of tempered judgement afterward. 480
ANGELO	I am sorry that such sorrow I procure;
	And so deep sticks it in my penitent heart
	That I crave death more willingly than mercy;
	'Tis my deserving, and I do entreat it.

Enter the PROVOST *with* BARNARDINE, CLAUDIO *(his face concealed)*
and JULIET.

DUKE	Which is that Barnardine?
PROVOST	This, my lord.
DUKE	There was a friar told me of this man.
	– Sirrah, thou art said to have a stubborn soul
	That apprehends no further than this world,
	And squar'st thy life according. Thou'rt condemned; 490
	But, for those earthly faults, I quit them all,
	And pray thee take this mercy to provide
	For better times to come. – Friar, advise him;
	I leave him to your hand. – What muffled fellow's that?
PROVOST	This is another prisoner that I saved,
	Who should have died when Claudio lost his head;
	As like almost to Claudio as himself.

                        [He reveals Claudio's face.

DUKE	[*to Isabella:*] If he be like your brother, for his sake
	Is he pardoned; and, for your lovely sake,
	Give me your hand, and say you will be mine. 500
	He is my brother too.[132] But fitter time for that.
	By this Lord Angelo perceives he's safe;
	Methinks I see a quick'ning in his eye.
	– Well, Angelo, your evil quits you well.
	Look that you love your wife: her worth, worth yours.
	I find an apt remission in myself;
	And yet here's one in place I cannot pardon.
	[*To Lucio:*] You, sirrah, that knew me for a fool, a
	coward,
	One all of luxury, an ass, a madman:
	Whérein have I so deserved of you 510
	That you extol me thus?
LUCIO	Faith, my lord, I spoke it but according to the trick. If

   you will hang me for it, you may; but I had rather it
   would please you I might be whipped.

DUKE Whipped first, sir, and hanged after.
   – Proclaim it, Provost, round about the city:
   If any woman wronged by this lewd fellow
   (As I have heard him swear himself there's one
   Whom he begot with child), let her appear,
   And he shall marry her. The nuptial finished,   520
   Let him be whipped and hanged.

LUCIO I beseech your Highness, do not marry me to a whore.
   Your Highness said even now I made you a duke; good
   my lord, do not recompense me in making me a cuckold.

DUKE Upon mine honour, thou shalt marry her.
   Thy slanders I forgive, and therewithal
   Remit thy other forfeits. – Take him to prison,
   And see our pleasure herein executed.

LUCIO Marrying a punk, my lord, is pressing to death, whip-
   ping, and hanging.   530

DUKE Slandering a prince deserves it.

         [*Exeunt officers with Lucio.*

   She, Claudio, that you wronged, look you restore.
   Joy to you, Mariana. Love her, Angelo;
   I have confessed her, and I know her virtue.
   Thanks, good friend Escalus, for thy much goodness;
   There's more behind that is more gratulate.
   Thanks, Provost, for thy care and secrecy;
   We shall employ thee in a worthier place.
   Forgive him, Angelo, that brought you home
   The head of Ragozine for Claudio's: 540
   Th'offence pardons itself. Dear Isabel,
   I have a motion much imports your good;
   Whereto if you'll a willing ear incline,
   What's mine is yours, and what is yours is mine.[133]
   So, bring us to our palace, where we'll show
   What's yet behind that's meet you all should know.

         [*Exeunt.*

FINIS.

NOTES ON *MEASURE FOR MEASURE*

In these notes, the abbreviations include the following:

cf.   *confer* (Latin): compare.

e.g.:   *exempli gratia* (Latin): for example;

F1:   the First Folio (1623);

F2:   the Second Folio (1632);

i.e.:   *id est* (Latin): that is, in other words;

O.E.D.:   *The Oxford English Dictionary* (2nd edition, 1989, and web-site);

S.D.:   stage-direction.

Biblical quotations are taken from the Geneva Bible (1560), though I have modernised the spellings.

In the case of a pun or an ambiguity, the meanings are distinguished as (a) and (b), or as (a), (b) and (c).

1 (Title) *MEAURE FOR MEASURE*: At 5.1.413–15, the Duke says: 'An Angelo for Claudio, death for death! . . . and measure still for measure!'. Here the words invoke retributive justice and bring to mind the Old Testament's harsh doctrine, 'life for life, eye for eye, tooth for tooth' (Exodus 21:23–4, Leviticus 24:17–20 and Deuteronomy 19:21). Nevertheless, the title-phrase may also invoke the New Testament's contrasting emphasis on mercy: 'Judge not, that ye be not judged. For with what judgement ye judge, ye shall be judged, and with what measure ye mete, it shall be measured to you again.' (Matthew 7:1–2; cf. Luke 6:37–8; though Mark 4:24–5 offers a sombre variant.)

2 (1.1.7–9) *Then . . . work.*: The sense is obscure, probably because the printer omitted some words. My conjectural reconstruction is: 'Then no more remains, / But that, to your sufficiency, you add / Such of my powers, as your worth is

able, / And let them work.' (I.e., 'Then all that remains is for you to add to your own abilities as much of my delegated power as your worthy self is able to, and set the combination to work.')

3 (1.1.35–6) *Spirits . . . issues;*: 'People are given sensitive souls only for fine actions;'.

4 (1.1.29–40) *Thyself . . . use.*:   This passage echoes various New Testament parables: e.g., Matthew 5:15, Mark 4:21–2, Luke 8:16–17, and particularly the parable of the talents in Matthew 25:14–30. The idea that virtue should be employed is, however, a proverbial commonplace of classical and Christian teachings.

5 (1.1.40–42) *But . . . Angelo;*: 'But I am directing my speech to someone who can publicly display what I confer on him. For that purpose, take this commission, Angelo:'.

6 (1.1.69–70) *Though . . . vehement;*: 'Although such actions are good, I do not greatly enjoy their loud applause and forceful cries of "*Ave*";'. (*Ave*, Latin for 'Be well' or 'Hail', was a salutation to Roman emperors and to St. Mary.)

7 (1.2.6–8) *Thou . . . table.*:   Of the Ten Commandments given to Moses by God (according to Exodus 20:1–17), the eighth is 'Thou shalt not steal'.

8 (1.2.26–32) *Well . . . now?*:   The first gentleman says that he and Lucio were cut from the same cloth: they are as bad as each other. Lucio replies that, on the contrary, he is like velvet, whereas the other man is like the plain edging of a piece of cloth. The gentleman responds that he would rather resemble English coarse cloth than be like Lucio, who is not so much a three-piled (rich) velvet as a thrice-peeled French velvet (alluding to the baldness resulting from the 'French disease', venereal disease, and from its treatment with mercury). 'Piled' resembles 'pilled' (i.e. 'peeled'). 'Feelingly' ('impressively') is taken by Lucio as 'painfully', implying that the gentleman has oral sores caused by disease.

9 (1.2.1–75) *If . . . custom-shrunk.*:   This material seems partly to duplicate what follows. Some editors speculate that these lines were added to Shakespeare's material by a different writer, but others disagree. The two accounts of Claudio's arrest (for example) may be regarded as complementary rather than con-

tradictory. Alternatively, apparent duplication may be a sign of unresolved revision by Shakespeare.

10 (1.2.81–3) *Groping . . . him.*:   Trout near a river-bank may be caught by someone who first 'tickles' them and then snatches them out. 'Peculiar' means 'privately owned'. Lucio implies that the arrested man enjoyed illicit sexual activity. Overdone asks whether a 'maid' is pregnant by him, but, as 'maid' can mean 'virgin', and a virgin (other than St. Mary) cannot be pregnant, Pompey corrects her. (The noun 'maid' is, however, used for the young, male or female, of some fish; and even a human male, if virginal, could be termed a 'maid'.)

11 (1.2.111–12) *The words . . . just.*:   Claudio likens Angelo to God, who, according to Romans 9:18, 'hath mercy on whom he will, & whom he will, he hardeneth'.

12 (1.2.156) *nineteen zodiacs*:   nineteen years; but at 1.3.21 the Duke specifies 'fourteen years'. (Shakespeare often errs when attempting to be numerically specific.)

13 (1.3.10) *Where . . . keeps.*:   'where young people and expense maintain a stupid ostentation.' In F1, the line seems unmetrically short, so some editors mend the metre by supplying (as here) an 'a' before 'witless'. The combination of a singular verb with a plural subject occurs from time to time in Shakespeare.

14 (1.3.20–21) *(The needful . . . sleep,*:   F1's version of line 20 ends with 'weedes', which many editors emend as 'steeds'. (Although *O.E.D.* says that 'weed' was a term for 'a poor, leggy, loosely-built horse', its earliest instance of this sense is dated 1845, and 'headstrong' implies vigour rather than weakness.) A possible alternative emendation is 'wills'. In line 21, F1's version ends with 'slip', but the emendation 'sleep' fits better the imagery of the unused 'biting laws' and the 'o'ergrown lion'.

15 (1.3.27) *Becomes . . . decrees,*:   In F1, the line is: 'More mock'd, then fear'd: so our Decrees,'. Perhaps the compositor over-looked a word or two.

16 (1.3.42–3) *And yet . . . slander.*:   'and yet I personally, never being involved in this fight against wickedness, cannot provoke slanderous accusations [e.g., of hypocrisy or gross inconsist-ency].' The phrase 'To do in slander' is odd, and may be corrupt.

17 (1.4.5) *Saint Clare.*:   The order of nuns ('The Poor Clares')

established by St. Clare of Assisi was very strict, with rules of
poverty, silence and abstinence.

18 (1.4.32) *to seem the lapwing,*:   The lapwing or peewit was said
to deceive potential raiders of its nest by making loud cries
when farthest from it; so the bird became associated with deceit
and hypocrisy.

19 (2.1.12) *the resolute . . . blood*:   Though some editors emend it as
'your', I retain F1's 'our', the meaning being then: 'resolutely
acting on sexual urges present in all men'.

20 (2.1.22–3) *What . . . thieves?*:   Either (a) 'What does the legal
system know of thieves in the jury passing sentence on thieves
in the dock?'; or (b) 'What body knows the laws that thieves
use to judge thieves?'. The former option, which fits the
context better, assumes that F1's phrasing again links a singular
verb to a plural subject.

21 (2.1.30–31) *Let . . . partial.*:   The meaning is probably: 'let my
previous judgement (the death-sentence) be applied to me, so
that it is in no way biased in my favour'; but 'Let . . . nothing
come in partial' could mean: 'let . . . nothing which is biased in
my favour intervene'.

22 (2.1.39–40) *Some . . . alone.*:   F1's version of line 39 begins:
'Some run from brakes of Ice'. The compositor perhaps made
an auditory error, his mind converting 'of Vice' to 'of Ice'. The
sense is: '[S]ome people run from thickets of vice and are not
held responsible (for their wickedness in there), while others
are condemned for a single fault.'

23 (2.1.46–9) *the poor . . . benefactors.*:   In Shakespeare's plays,
constables usually mangle the language: Elbow resembles Dull
in *Love's Labour's Lost* and Dogberry and Verges in *Much Ado
about Nothing*. Here 'poor Duke's constable' should be 'Duke's
poor constable', 'lean upon justice' (rely on justice) unwittingly
mocks his name, and 'benefactors' should be 'malefactors'. (The
Glossary includes other blunders.)

24 (2.1.86) *stewed prunes*:   As 'stew' meant 'brothel', stewed
prunes may have been a brothel-signal as well as a snack
supplied there. Thomas Dekker's *The Seuen Deadly Sinnes of
London* (1606), p. 21, says that at houses of ill-repute in the
London suburbs, 'they set stewed Prunes befor[e] you'.

25 (2.1.112–14) *Come . . . not.*:   Escalus means: 'Come to the

point: tell me what was done to her.' Pompey wilfully takes him to mean 'Let me experience what was done to her' (or perhaps 'Let me have an orgasm while hearing what was done to her'). Escalus repudiates such misinterpretation.

26 (2.1.164) *Hannibal!*:   Elbow thinks of Pompey as a cannibal (for, metaphorically, he feeds on human flesh), but confuses 'cannibal' with 'Hannibal', a confusion augmented by the fact that the famous Pompey was, like Hannibal, a great general.

27 (2.1.188) *Overdone . . . last.*:   He means both (a) 'She gained the surname "Overdone" by her most recent marriage.', and (b) 'She was worn out sexually by her last husband.'.

28 (2.1.191–2) *they will . . . them.*:   The word 'draw' could mean 'draw in', 'draw drink for someone', 'drain of money', 'drag to execution' and 'disembowel', while 'hang them' means 'cause them to be hanged' (for tricking and robbing Froth). Escalus is thinking particularly of malefactors who are 'hung (or hanged), drawn and quartered'.

29 (2.1.228–30) *I shall . . . you*::   Plutarch says that at the battle of Pharsalia (48 B.C.), Pompey the Great retreated to his tent when he realised that Julius Cæsar had defeated him.

30 (2.2.10–11) *Why . . . rash*::   Here, and on numerous subsequent occasions in F1, one line of trimeter (six syllables in three iambic feet) is followed in dialogue by a second such line from the next speaker. Some editors combine them as a single Alexandrine (one line of hexameter, twelve syllables in six iambic feet). I generally follow F1 in keeping them as two short lines.

31 (2.2.29–30) *There . . . Honour!*:   A parliamentary Act of 1606 forbade the use of God's name in staged plays. It is highly probable, though not certain, that the text of *Measure for Measure* was affected by consequent censorship. If, for instance, ''Save your Honour!' had originally been 'God save your Honour!' (as F1's apostrophe may hint), the words from 'There' to 'Honour!' would make a line of iambic pentameter. At 2.2.170, the addition of 'God' similarly improves the metre; and, at 2.4.4, replacement of 'Heaven' by 'God' enhances both the metre and the sense.

32 (2.2.64) *May . . . this*::   In F1, the line is short: 'May call it againe: well, beleeue this'. F2 mends the metre by inserting 'back' after 'it'.

33 (2.2.71–2) *he . . . stern.*:   'he, if he had been in your position as
    deputy, would have been more lenient than you are.'

34 (2.2.79–85) *Why . . . new-made.*:   Isabella invokes the Christian
    doctrine that, though all people were once destined to be
    damned, God, instead of seizing the penal opportunity,
    remedied their plight by sending Jesus Christ as a sacrifice to
    atone for human sin. As we are all sinners, she proceeds, we are
    all dependent for our salvation on God's mercy. Therefore,
    Angelo should himself be merciful. The phrasing of 'mercy
    then will breathe within your lips / Like man new-made'
    recalls partly the creation of Adam (Genesis 2:7) and partly the
    Biblical assurances of regeneration (e.g., 2 Corinthians 5:17 and
    Ephesians 2:4–6, 4:21–4).

35 (2.2.102–5) *Either . . . end.*:   Where F1 has 'Either now, or',
    editors have suggested various emendations, e.g. 'Either new
    or' (as here), 'Or new, or', 'Either now born', 'Either raw, or'
    and 'Eggs now, or'. In line 105, 'ere' emends F1's 'here'.

36 (2.2.120–23) *Merciful . . . myrtle.*:   Jove (and the skies) send
    thunderbolts, but Heaven is merciful in cleaving the powerful
    oak (which is knotty and invulnerable to splitting by wedges)
    rather than the soft myrtle. The myrtle is 'soft' because it is
    relatively weak and is vulnerable to cold, but perhaps also
    because it is a plant sacred to Venus and emblematic of love – in
    contrast to the oak, which is emblematic of strength. (In line
    122, 'Splits', instead of 'Splittest' or 'Splitt'st', illustrates a class
    of inconsistency found elsewhere in F1.)

37 (2.2.123–9) *But . . . mortal.*:   The 'glassy essence' is probably
    the soul (which, like transparent glass, is hard to perceive) or
    possibly individual life (which is fragile as glass). Proud man
    resembles an angry ape in imitating God and playing bizarre
    pranks in the sight of Heaven, so that the angels weep; whereas,
    if angels had spleens as we do (spleens being the source of both
    wrath and mirth), they would respond by laughing themselves
    either to death or into the condition of human beings.

38 (2.2.132) *We . . . self.*:   'We should not weigh our fellow-
    human with ourselves', for great people are judged more
    leniently than lesser people. Isabella next gives illustrations of
    this double standard (great men may jest about holy people, an
    oath from an officer will be condoned), but then criticises it,

claiming that authority can superficially conceal vice; and she proceeds to say that if Angelo finds that he conceals sexual desires like Claudio's, he should be merciful.

39 (2.2.147–52) *She . . . me?*:   Angelo's 'Such sense that my sense breeds with it' means 'so cogently (on the topic of sexuality) that she makes my sexual desires burgeon'. Her offer of a bribe probably makes him suspect a sexual offer.

40 (2.2.170) *Save . . . Honour!*:   Her parting salutation means 'May God preserve your honourable self!'; but Angelo sees an unintended meaning: 'May God preserve your moral honour from corruption by dishonourable conduct with the seductively virtuous Isabella!'.

41 (2.2.173–6) *it is I . . . season.*:   'it is I, who, lying by the (fragrant and demure) violet in the sunshine, act like rotting flesh, not like the flower: paradoxically, the healthy, sunny season (and the beneficent seasoning of the violet's perfume) corrupt me.'

42 (2.2.177–80) *betray . . . there?*:   The phrase 'betray our sense' can mean (a) 'elicit our lust' and '(b) 'betray our good sense'; 'the sanctuary' means (a) 'some sacred place' and (b) 'virginity'; while 'pitch our evils' can mean (a) 'cast our urine and fæces', (b) 'erect privies', (c) 'establish our vices', and (d) 'have sinful sexual ejaculations'.

43 (2.2.188–9) *O . . . hook!*:   The 'cunning enemy' is Satan, who sometimes tempted saints or hermits by appearing in the guise of another saint or a virtuous woman.

44 (2.3.4–5) *I come . . . prison.*:   Cf. 1 Peter 3:19, which says that Jesus 'preached unto the spirits that were in prison'.

45 (2.3.28) *Then . . . his.*:   The Duke takes a masculist view that, though the sexual act is mutual, the woman is more culpable than the male for permitting it. This was not an orthodoxy at the time. Some writers (also masculist) held that the male, being more rational, was guiltier. In *The Tempest*, Prospero will specifically warn Ferdinand against breaching Miranda's virginity before marriage. (Jesus, of course, declined to condemn the adulterous woman: John 8:3–11.)

46 (2.3.30–34) *lest . . . fear–*:   The Duke insists that she should be penitent not because the sin has brought her to shame (which would be a selfish reason) but because it entails opposition to God.

47 (2.3.41–3) *O . . . horror!*:   Following F1, I retain 'love', which
yields the following sense: 'O harmful love, which, by resulting
in pregnancy, spares my life, the comfort of which (Claudio's
love for me) entails a recognition of the horror of death (the
knowledge that Claudio must die).' The main implication is
that her pregnancy has won her a reprieve from the death-
sentence. Some editors prefer to change 'love' to 'law', so that
she sees the law which spares her life as both harmful and unjust
(as she must suffer the loss of Claudio).

48 (2.4.7–9) *The state . . . tedious;*:   Here, 'state' means either (a)
'condition, rôle in life' or (b) 'statecraft, politics'. In line 9, F1
has 'feard' (i.e. 'feared'), but the emendation 'seared' ('dried up
or withered') makes better sense.

49 (2.4.16–17) *Let's . . . crest.*:   In spite of the name that he bears,
Angelo ('the angel'), thought to be so pure, has discovered
wickedness within himself; so he bitterly suggests that a
similar paradox applies to the devil. The horn may no longer
be the distinguishing crest of the devil, but may identify a
good angel, so we should write 'good angel' on that horn.
Some editors emend 'not' as 'now', so that the 'crest' is the
inscription rather than the horn. (Matthew 25:41 shows that
an angel could be evil.)

50 (2.4.32–3) *That . . . 'tis.*:   'You ask what my pleasure (i.e. my
decision about Claudio) is. I would much rather that instead of
asking my pleasure, you knew (experienced) it.' (His pleasure
would lie in copulating with her.) Many editors mark these
words as an aside (F1 does not; indeed, it customarily does not
specify asides); but Angelo's phrasing is sufficiently obscure for
them to be uttered directly to her. As yet, Isabella has no
suspicion of Angelo's ulterior motive. She could take the
words to mean: 'It would be far less unpleasant for me if you
knew the bad news (about Claudio) already, instead of asking
me to tell it to you.'

51 (2.4.41–5) *It were . . . forbid.*:   'It would be as good to pardon
a person guilty of murder as to pardon the impudent delectation
of those who (like forgers of coins) create an illegitimate child.'
The phrase 'Heaven's image' may be a censored version of
'God's image', for Genesis 1:26–7 tells how 'God created the
man in his own image'. In *Cymbeline*, Act 2, scene 5, Shakespeare

again likens the begetting of illegitimate children to the
counterfeiting of coins.

52 (2.4.52) *or . . . him,*: Here, 'or' is a standard emendation of
F1's 'and'.

53 (2.4.56–7) *our . . . accompt.*: This is proverbial: 'Compelled
sins are no sins.' It is also a crucial point which Isabella later
neglects.

54 (2.4.74–5) *craftily . . . nothing good*: Here, 'craftily' is an
emendation of F1's 'crafty', and 'me' is absent from F1 but
present in F2.

55 (2.4.88–9) *(As . . . question,*: In F1 the closing bracket follows
'question'. The emendation offers the following meaning:
'(not that I agree to this or any other way), except, assuming
you lost your argument,'. Later, in line 93, 'all-binding'
emends F1's 'all-building'.

56 (2.4.99–108) *were I . . . ever.*: The erotic element in lines 99–
103 is striking and apt. The phrase 'longing have' may possibly
be a Shakespearian combination of singular subject and plural
verb, or it may be a compression of 'longing I have'. At 104-8,
she assumes that her sexual submission would entail her eternal
damnation, although the deed, if not enjoyed by her, would
resemble a martyrdom and might even help her to become a
saint.

57 (2.4.131) *credulous . . . prints.*: 'as soft metal can easily be
moulded by the forger, so we can be led astray by a seducer.';
or, more simply, 'easily deceived.'.

58 (2.4.133–4) *(Since . . . frames),*: '(as, I imagine, we are not
made to be invulnerable to sinful temptations),'.

59 (2.4.159–60) *you . . . calumny.*: 'your own allegation will
smother you, and you will reek as a slanderer.'

60 (3.1.13–15) *Thou . . . baseness.*: 'You are not noble, because
all the comforts that you carry about with you (your clothing
and adornments) have low origins.'

61 (3.1.17–19) *The best . . . more.*: 'Sleep, which you often
solicit, is the best form of rest, and yet you greatly (or stupidly)
fear your death, which is no more than sleep.' The 'Friar' is
here offering a pagan (Epicurean) doctrine, in contrast to the
Christian doctrine of an afterlife in which there may be eternal
torture.

62 (3.1.23–5) *Thou . . . moon.*: 'You are not consistent and reliable, because your temperament veers (like the ever-changing moon), with strange consequences.'

63 (3.1.29–32) *thine . . . sooner.*: 'the true issue of your own loins and genitals, the children who call you "father", curse the gout, the serpigo and the watery excesses of your body for not killing you sooner.' In line 29, 'thee "Sire" ' is an emendation of F1's 'thee, fire'. 'Sapego' (F1) or 'serpigo' is a spreading skin-disease.

64 (3.1.41–3) *That . . . life.*: 'That makes these odds all even' means 'which resolves these paradoxes' or 'which levels all these differences'. Claudio's resolution may echo Matthew 16:25: 'For whosoever will save his life, shall lose it: and whosoever shall lose his life for my sake, shall find it.'

65 (3.1.78–80) *the poor . . . dies.*:   She intends to say that the death of a giant entails no more bodily suffering than does that of a humble beetle, but the sense of her phrasing is the opposite: the poor trodden beetle suffers as greatly as a dying giant.

66 (3.1.91–2) *follies . . . fowl,*:   F1's 'enmew' means 'mew up or confine'; loosely, 'hem in'. A possible emendation is 'enew', meaning 'drive into the water'; loosely, 'repel'.

67 (3.1.95) *princely Angelo?*:   Here and in line 98, F1 has 'prenzie', a word which, according to *O.E.D.*, is 'doubtful . . . ; prob[ably] an error'. In 1632, F2 emended it as 'princely'. Some editors prefer 'precise', but this word is metrically inappropriate, as the rhythm solicits a trochee (such as '*prince*ly') rather than an iamb ('pre*cise*'). Line 98's 'princely guards' are 'rich fabrics fronting garments'. So, in 95, 'princely' means 'authoritarian, behaving like a ruler', and, in 98, it means 'suitable for a ruler, rich'.

68 (3.1.101–2) *he . . . still.*: 'as a consequence of this foul sin, he would give you the opportunity to continue to offend him'.

69 (3.1.110–13) *Has . . . least.*: 'Does he really have desires so strong that they can make him treat with contempt the very law which he is supposed to be enforcing? Surely, of the seven deadly sins, it (lust) is the least important.' The seven deadly sins are pride, wrath, envy, lust, gluttony, avarice and sloth.

70 (3.1.120–34) *Ay . . . death.*:   Here, 'Obstruction', 'sensible' and 'warm motion' mean (respectively) 'constriction', 'sensitive' and 'warm and mobile living body'. The spirit is 'delighted' in the

sense (probably) of 'delightable': in life it has a capacity to experience delight or be delightful, although (in Claudio's imagination) it is doomed to suffer post-mortal torments. Possible emendations include 'dilated' ('dispersed') and 'delated' ('accused of wrong-doing'). 'To bathe' is F2's emendation of F1's 'To bath'; 'thrilling' means 'piercingly cold'; 'regions' is a common emendation of F1's 'region'; and 'viewless' means 'invisible'. The 'lawless and incertain thoughts' may include (a) conjectures about the sufferings of souls in Purgatory, a location abolished by Protestantism, or (b) the imaginings of Hell and Purgatory by such Catholics as Dante. To fit the plural verb, 'thoughts' emends F1's 'thought'; and 'penury' is F2's emendation of F1's 'periury'. The imagery of this passage combines details of classical and Christian eschatology, as found, for example, in Virgil's *Æneid* and Dante's *Inferno*; particularly *Inferno* 5:28–51, in which wailing 'carnal sinners' are blown about in warring winds.

71 (3.1.141–5) *Is't . . . blood.*: She thinks that if her sexual act gave life to a brother, it would be as if she had committed incest (with her father). 'Heaven shield' means 'Heaven forbid that'. '[A] warpèd slip of wilderness' suggests both (a) 'a contorted cutting from a wild plant' and (b) 'a corrupt descendant of licentiousness'.

72 (3.1.175–80) *Provost . . . time.*: This apparently pointless exchange between the Duke and the Provost may have been designed to give Claudio time to effect some reconciliation with Isabella. (F1 predictably gives no stage-direction equivalent to '*Claudio joins Isabella*', nor does it provide an exit for Claudio after the Duke says 'Farewell' to him.)

73 (3.1.182–4) *the goodness . . . fair.*: 'if goodness is little valued by a beautiful person, that beauty soon declines; but, as divinely-granted virtue is the essence of your character, your body will always retain its beauty.'

74 (3.1.244–6) *place . . . time . . . convenience.*: F1 reverses the order of the nouns 'place' and 'time'.

75 (3.2.) SCENE 2.: Though numerous editors provide one, F1 does not provide a scene-division here, and this scene can be performed as a continuation of the previous one, the Duke remaining on stage. Nevertheless, the specified change of

location suits the action (and such injunctions as 'Take him to prison, officer' and 'Go, away with her to prison').

76 (3.2.3–4) *drink . . . bastard.*: 'drink red and white sweet Spanish wine' (and, it is implied, become accustomed to brown and white illegitimate children).

77 (3.2.9–10) *craft . . . facing.*: 'cunning, being wealthier than innocence, provides the rich frontage of the garment.' (The fur of the cunning fox covers the skin of the innocent lamb.) The noun 'facing' could also mean 'outfacing' or 'effrontery'. In line 9, 'on' is an emendation of F1's 'and'.

78 (3.2.11) *father friar.*: As 'friar' means 'brother', Elbow's phrase invites the Duke's retort.

79 (3.2.30) *prove his.*: 'prove to be his agent.'

80 (3.2.34–9) *if he . . . sir.*: Elbow's 'as good go a mile on his errand' means 'it would be better for him to be a mile away', but he ludicrously puts this after 'and comes before him'. Elbow's remark about 'your waist' means that, as the waist of the 'friar' is encircled by a cord, Pompey's neck will soon be encircled by a hangman's noose.

81 (3.2.42–50) *How . . . of it?*: The gist of this badinage is: 'Are you downcast, and have nothing to say for yourself?'. Pompey the Great was defeated by Julius Cæsar; captives of Roman rulers were led in triumphal processions through Rome; Pygmalion's statue of a beautiful woman was given life by Venus, and here is likened to a attractive whore.

82 (3.2.55) *tub.*: Having eaten all the salted beef that it contained, she is now (allegedly) using the tub as a powdering-tub, in which a person suffering from venereal disease would be fumigated (e.g. by cinnabar, mercuric sulphide).

83 (3.2.71–2) *If . . . more.*: A standard pun (mettle/metal). Pompey's mettle (spirit, courage) will be greater, and so will the weight of metal (in the fetters) that he bears.

84 (3.2.77–8) *then . . . now.*: Pompey's 'then' means 'therefore' ('because I am in need of it'); Lucio's 'then' is temporal ('neither in the past nor now').

85 (3.2.104–6) *And . . . apace.*: 'And he is a sexless puppet; that's certain.' 'You are jocular, sir, and gabble.' (F1 has 'generatiue', but 'ungenerative' fits better; cf. 'ungenitured' in line 161.)

86 (3.2.140–41) *Love . . . love.*: 'If you really loved him, you would

be better informed; and if you knew more of him, you would love him more fully.' (In line 141, 'dearer' is an emendation of FI's 'deare'.)

87 (3.2.168–9) *eat . . . Fridays*.:   (a) break the ecclesiastical law that fish and not meat was to be consumed on Friday; (b) enjoy a prostitute on a day of (dietary) abstinence.

88 (3.2.188) *Philip and Jacob*;:   May 1, the festival of Saints Philip and James.

89 (3.2.208–11) *Novelty . . . undertaking*.:   'Only new things are in demand; and, in the present situation, it is as perilous to be long-established in any kind of activity as it is virtuous to be variable in any undertaking.' In line 210, 'inconstant' is an emendation of FI's 'constant'.

90 (3.2.232–3) *You . . . calling*.:   'You have served Heaven as you should, and have fulfilled to the utmost the duty of a friar to the prisoner.'

91 (3.2.236) *he is . . . Justice*.:   'he behaves like the incarnate idea of pure Justice, distinct from Mercy.'

92 (3.2.245–7) *Grace . . . weighing*.:   'possessing the divinely-granted grace to withstand evil, as well as the virtue to go into action; being no more severe or lenient to others than is compatible with knowledge of his own culpability.'

93 (3.2.254–7) *How may . . . things?*:   This is a notorious crux: the passage appears corrupt, and probably a couplet is missing. As they stand, the incoherent lines seem to mean: 'How may a similarity in criminality, deceiving people these days, . . . to pull weighty and substantial matters with trivial spiders' threads?'. One unifying (if strained) suggestion is that FI's 'To draw' should be 'To-draw' (i.e. 'pull to itself ').

94 (3.2.242–63) *He . . . contracting*.:   This speech, in sententious couplets of tetrameter, has led some editors to speculate (a) that it is the work of a reviser, or (b) that an adaptor transposed it with that at 4.1.59–64, or (c) that it was shorn of the lines which became 4.1.59–64.

95 (4.1. S.D.) *a singing BOY*.:   Some editors conjecture that the song and part of the subsequent material of this scene were added by an adaptor; but the provision of a lyrical interlude is characteristically Shakespearian.

96 (4.1.3–4) *those . . . morn*;:   'your eyes, which, at break of day,

light up so brightly that the misled morning thinks they are the sun;'. The song about a woman betrayed in love is obviously appropriate to Mariana's plight. My hyphens in 'break-of-day' clarify the adjectival status of the phrase.

97 (4.1.53) *Good . . . it.*:   Some editors mend the metre of F1's version by adding 'so' after 'and'; but strong stress on 'you' can regulate the line: 'Good fríar, Ì know *yóu* do, ànd have fóund it.'.

98 (4.1.59–64) *O place . . . fancies.*:   In line 61, 'contrarious' means (a) 'perverse', (b) 'inconsistent' and (c) 'hostile'. F2 converts to a plural F1's 'quest' (which can mean both 'pursuit' and 'the barking of hunting-dogs in sight of game'). The 'escapes' are sallies. The closing idea is that numerous people waste their intelligence on idle fancies which are supposedly true accounts of the authoritative person, and thus, in and by their imaginations, torture and distort him. (Some editors conjecture that this soliloquy was originally part of an earlier one in Act 3, scene 2.)

99 (4.1.72–7) *Nor . . . sow.*:   The Duke's argument in lines 72–6 contradicts what he said to Juliet in Act 2, scene 3. A 'tithe' is rent to be paid in the form of one-tenth of the yield of crops. Some editors depart from F1 to emend 'tithe' as 'tilth' ('tillage, arable land, ploughed field').

100 (4.2.2–4) *if he . . . head.*:   'For the husband is the wife's head': Ephesians 5:23.

101 (4.2.39–43) *Every . . . thief.*:   'Every honest man's clothing satisfies the thief of it.' 'If the outfit is too small for the thief, the honest man still thinks it big enough (a sufficiently big loss); if it is too big for the thief, the thief thinks it little enough (a small reward for his risky venture).' (The hangman's perquisite was the clothing of his victim; so the thief was, in effect, the tailor of the hangman.) I follow F1 in allocating lines 40–43 to Pompey, but some editors allocate them to Abhorson.

102 (4.2.45–7) *I do . . . forgiveness.*:   The hangman was supposed to request the forgiveness of the man about to be hanged.

103 (4.2.54) *good turn.*:   Pompey is ironic, 'good turn' meaning (a) 'favour' and (b) 'thorough hanging'.

104 (4.2.84–6) *That . . . up.*:   In line 84, 'unshifting' is an

emendation of F1's 'unsisting'. Lines 85–6 reveal that the Provost had gone out to call an officer to admit the person knocking.

105 (4.2.95) *This . . . man.*:   Here, F1 has 'This is his Lords man.', attributed to the Duke. The next line is attributed by F1 (implausibly) to the Provost.

106 (4.2.138–39) *insensible . . . mortal.*:   'unaware of the reality of death, and hopelessly mortal (i.e., merely human, destined to death, and perhaps without hope of salvation).'

107 (4.3.3–8) *First . . . dead.*:   'Master Rash' and the other customers have allegoric names which erode the distinction between Vienna and England. (Among the ensuing names, 'Forthright' emends F1's 'Forthlight'.) Rash is the victim of a money-lender. In England, as the legal rate of interest was usually limited to 10%, a usurer might insist that the borrower take part of the loan in the form of 'a commodity', overpriced goods of little value (e.g. brown paper). Apparently, Rash has incurred a debt of £197 on the goods but gained little more than £3 in cash for them.

108 (4.3.17–18) *are . . . sake'.*:   'For the Lord's sake' was a cry of prisoners as they begged for food.

109 (4.3.59) *After . . . block.*:   I follow F1 in allocating this line to the Duke. Some editors re-allocate it to the Provost, to make the Duke's conduct seem less erratic; but the Duke hopes to persuade Barnardine to die 'willingly' (line 75).

110 (4.3.82–3) *Ere . . . generation,*:   Probably: 'Before the sun has twice made his daily greeting to all those living outside the prison,': i.e. 'Within two days,'. (Here, 'yonder' emends F1's 'yond'.)

111 (4.3.87) *Varrius –*:   F1 has 'Angelo', but this is probably an error for 'Varrius', as Angelo is to meet the Duke not at the fountain but at the city gates (see line 125).

112 (4.3. S.D. after 95) *Enter . . . box.*:   In F1, the S.D. is simply '*Enter the Prouost.*'. I provide the box in the interests of hygiene, economy and tidiness, and to make 'Here is the head' less comically tautological.

113 (4.3.122) *One . . . cónfessor,*:   I follow F1's 'couent' (i.e. 'covent'), a variant of 'convent'. In this line, as probably in 2.1.35 and elsewhere in Shakespeare, 'confessor' is scanned

'*cón*-fess-òr'. This particular confessor was 'Friar Thomas' in Act 1, scene 3, but soon he becomes 'Friar Peter'. (In Act 1, scene 2, Pompey was greeted as 'Thomas'.)

114 (4.3.147–8) *I dare . . . to't.*:   'I dare not eat well, for one rich meal would impel me to lechery, which might cost me my head.'

115 (4.3.150–51) *If . . . lived.*:   The title 'Duke of Dark Corners' recalls the Latin proverb (cited in the source-play *Promos and Cassandra*), '*Veritas non querit angulos*': 'Truth does not seek [dark] corners'.

116 (4.4.5) *re-deliver . . . there?*:   Here, 're-deliver' emends F1's 're-/liuer'.

117 (4.4.13–15) *Well . . . him.*:   I follow F1 in setting the lines as prose. Some editors re-set them as verse, but it seems more logical to preserve the shift to verse at line 18.

118 (4.4.24) *a . . . bulk,*:   'such strong credibility'. Here, 'a so' emends F1's 'of a'.

119 (4.4.27–8) *Save . . . revenge,*:   'except that his youthful wildness, full of fierce urges, might in future have taken revenge,'. The 'revenge' considered is almost certainly against Angelo (who is here assessing threats to himself), rather than against Claudio.

120 (4.5. S.D.) Outside the city.:   F1, as usual, does not specify the location. Some editors suggest that the location is a friar's cell; others, recalling the Duke's intention to proceed to the city gates from 'the consecrated fount' (4.3.92), prefer a location outside the city.

121 (4.5.5–6) *Though . . . house,*:   'though sometimes you may veer from this argument to that as occasion arises. Go, call at Flavius' house,'. 'Flavius'' emends F1's '*Flauia*'s'.

122 (5.1.47–8) *truth is . . . reck'ning.*:   Cf. 1 Esdras 4:38: 'But truth doth abide, and is strong forever, and liveth and reigneth for ever and ever.'

123 (5.1.67) *inequality;*:   She refers to either (a) the inequality in rank between herself and Angelo, or (b) the disparity between her allegation and the apparent truth.

124 (5.1.185–6) *I would . . . himself.*:   'I wish he had grounds (as a defendant) for his prattling.'

125 (5.1.188–91) *I do . . . me.*:   She can claim that Angelo is her

husband, because (although there has been no marriage ceremony), he was engaged to her and has subsequently copulated with her. Lines 190–91 mean: 'I have known my husband carnally; but he is unaware that he has had carnal knowledge of me.'

126 (5.1.295–6) *Respect . . . throne.*: 'Let respect be shown to your great position, Lord Escalus; and, as for Lord Angelo, even the Devil deserves some respect for being the ruler of flaming Hell.'

127 (5.1.317–18) *his . . . provincial.*: 'I am a subject neither of the Duke nor of the ecclesiastical authorities here.'

128 (5.1.323–4) *forfeits . . . mark:*:   Apparently the allusion is to jocular forfeits, fines paid for such minor misdemeanours as swearing; so they would be objects of mirth rather than warnings to be heeded.

129 (5.1.408–10) *double . . . life,*:   Angelo has perhaps committed a 'double violation' of sacred chastity by threatening Isabella's and taking Mariana's; and he has broken his promise to spare Claudio's life in return.

130 (5.1.413–15) *death for . . . measure!'*: 'Death for death' and 'Measure for measure' are proverbial phrases. (Cf. Exodus 21:23–5.) In contrast, Jesus opposed the doctrine of 'an eye for an eye', declaring: 'Love your enemies: . . . and pray for them which hurt you, and persecute you.' (See Matthew 5:38–45.)

131 (5.1.457–8) *Thoughts . . . thoughts.*:   'Thoughts are not subject to the law, and intentions are no more than thoughts.' She contradicts Jesus' claim that 'whosoever looketh on a woman to lust after her, hath committed adultery with her already in his heart.' (Matthew 5:27–8.)

132 (5.1.501) *He . . . too.*: 'Then (assuming that you agree) he becomes my brother (brother-in-law).'

133 (5.1.544) *What's . . . is mine.*:   proverbial, and perhaps echoing the vows of mutuality in the Christian marriage service.

GLOSSARY

Where a pun, a metaphor or an ambiguity occurs, the meanings are distinguished as (a) and (b), or (a), (b) and (c), etc. Otherwise, alternative meanings are distinguished as (i) and (ii), or as (i), (ii) and (iii), etc. Abbreviations include the following: adj., adjective; adv., adverb; e.g., for example; interj., interjection; It., Italian; *O.E.D.*, *Oxford English Dictionary*; vb., verb.

able: 1.1.8: capable.

Abhorson: 'Abhorrent Son of a Whore'.

absolute: 5.1.56: (a) perfect; (b) untainted; (c) imperious.

accidental: 3.1.151: casual.

accommodation: 3.1.14: (a) comfort; (b) aid to life.

accompt: **more for number than accompt**: to add a numerical show rather than significance.

act (noun): 1.4.64: statute.

adjudge: 5.1.407: condemn.

admit: 2.4.87: suppose.

adoptedly: by choice.

advértise: instruct, inform.

advice: deliberation.

affect: (i: 1.1.4:) be too fond of; (ii: 1.1.72:) like, love.

affection: 2.1.10: desire.

affianced: betrothed, contracted.

again: 3.2.155: next time.

agèd: **as agèd**: 3.1.35: like an old beggar.

agent: 3.2.162: deputy.

All-hallond Eve: All Hallows' Eve, Oct. 31st.

and: 2.1.152; 5.1.78: if.

anon: very soon.

answer: **your answer**: 2.4.72: your responsibility.

answered: **darkly answered**: privately requited.

appliance: **in base appliances**: by low remedies.

approbation: (i: 1.2.166:) approval as a novitiate; (ii: 5.1.249:) approval.

arraign: 2.3.21: (a) accuse; (b) interrogate.

arrest: 2.4.135: (a) seize;
　(b) halt.

assay: try, test.

athwart: askew.

attorneyed: employed as an
　agent.

avail: 3.1.232: benefit.

Aves: cries of '*Ave*!' (Latin,
　'Hail!'): acclamations.

avised: 2.2.138: (a) advised;
　(b) aware.

avouch: vouch for.

bane: poison.

bared: 4.2.169: shorn.

bastard: 3.2.4: sweet Spanish
　wine.

battery: 2.1.168: (error for)
　slander.

bawd: (i: 3.2.18, 63, 65:)
　pimp; (ii: 3.2.57:) procuress;
　bawd born: 3.2.66: (a) born
　to be a pimp; (b) born of a
　procuress.

bay: 2.1.223: (a) space under
　gable; (b) space between two
　party-walls (*O.E.D.*).

behind: (i: 5.1.536:) to come;
　(ii: 5.1.546:) unknown to you.

belongings: attributes.

bend (vb.): 1.1.40: direct.

benedicite: (God) bless you.

betimes: early.

billet: 4.3.50: (a) cudgel;
　(b) log.

bitter: 4.2.73: cruel.

blasting: blighting.

blench: veer.

blessèd: 3.1.34: blissful, happy.

blood: 2.1.12: sexual desire.

bolt (noun): (i: 2.2.121:)
　thunderbolt; (ii: 5.1.347:)
　fetter.

boot: **with boot**: profitably.

borne up: 4.1.46: maintained.

bosom: (i: 4.3.128:) desire;
　(ii: 5.1.11: a) feelings;
　(b) appreciation.

bottom of my place: basis of
　my authority.

bowels: 3.1.29: offspring.

brain (vb.): kill.

bravery: **witless bravery**:
　stupid ostentation.

brawling: clamorous.

breed (vb.): 2.2.148: burgeon.

bruise (vb.): crush.

bulk: **credent bulk**: strong
　credibility.

burr: small prickly seed-head.

by and by: presently.

Cæsar: Julius Cæsar, who
　defeated Pompey.

caitiff: villain.

call upon: 3.2.147: challenge.

calumny: slander.

Caper: Frolic.

caracts: insignia.

cardinally: (error for) carnally.

carman: carter.

case: 2.4.13: garb.

cause: (i: 2.1.129–30: a) law-
　case; (b) reason;
　(ii: 2.2.1:) law-case.

ceremony: 2.2.65: sign of power.

change: 1.4.47: exchange.

character: (i: 1.1.27:) writing-
　style; (ii: 1.2.143; 4.2.184:)
　handwriting.

cipher: zero, empty sign.

circummured: walled round.

clack-dish: begging-bowl.

clap into: briskly begin.

close (vb.): conclude.

close (adj.): 4.3.112: silent.

clutched: 3.2.46: clenched (on money).

cod-piece: on hose or breeches, pouch for genitals.

combinate: pledged.

combinèd: bound.

comes off well: turns out well.

commodity: 4.3.4: item to facilitate usury.

common: public; **common ear**: public hearing; **common house**: brothel. **commonweal**: state.

cómplete: 1.3.3: fully equipped.

complexion: 3.1.24, 184: temperament.

composition: (i: 1.2.1–2:) agreement; (ii: 5.1.223:) the agreed sum.

compound (vb.): 4.2.20: agree terms.

conception: 2.4.7: devising.

concupiscible: sexually intense.

confederate companion: complicit hanger-on.

confessed her: 5.1.534: heard her confession.

confute: 5.1.104: (a) overcome; (b) convince.

congealed ice: frozen into icicles.

conjure: formally enjoin.

constantly: unfailingly.

consummate: completed.

continue: 2.1.178: (mistaken for) contain, i.e. be continent.

contrarious: 4.1.61: (a) perverse; (b) inconsistent; (c) hostile.

convénted: summoned.

Copper-Spur: (perhaps) Pretentious.

cost: 1.3.10: extravagance.

countenance (noun): 5.1.122: (a) ducal favour; (b) false appearance.

countenance (vb.): 5.1.322: condone.

covent: 4.3.122: convent.

covert bosom: hidden feelings.

crabbed: harsh.

cross (vb.): (i: 2.2.167:) conflict; (ii: 4.2.161:) oppose.

crotchet: eccentricity.

crown: **French crown**: (a) French gold coin; (b) baldness caused by syphilis.

cucullus non facit monachum (Latin): the cowl does not make a monk.

darkly: 5.1.282–3: (a) deviously; (b) in the dark.

Deep-Vow: Love-Pledger.

defiance: 3.1.145: (a) enmity; (b) disowning.

delighted: 3.1.123: (a) delightful; (b) capable of delight.

deliver: 4.2.119: reveal.

deliverance: release.

denunciation: formal announcement.

dependant: 4.3.85: servant.

deputation: 1.1.20: deputyship.

detected for women: 3.2.114: (a) suspected of womanising; (b) found to be a womaniser.

detest: 2.1.66, 71: (error for) attest.

device: 4.4.11: plot.

dinner: mid-day meal.

discover: (i: 3.1.194:) reveal, expose; (ii: 4.2.165:) recognise.

dislike: 1.2.16: express aversion to.

dispatch: 3.1.263: agree promptly.

distant: 2.1.87: (error for) instant.

disvouch: contradict.

Dizzy: Foolish.

dolours: 1.2.44: (a) griefs; (b) dollars, sums of money.

dower: dowry.

drab (noun): whore.

drawn in: 2.1.194: (a) enticed in; (b) cheated.

dressings: 5.1.58: ceremonial attire.

dribbling dart: feeble arrow.

Drop-Heir: 4.3.14: (perhaps: a) Parasite; (b) Kill-Heir.

ducat: gold or silver coin.

durance: **perpetual durance**: a life sentence.

edge: 1.4.60: sexual urge.

effect: 2.1.13: fulfilment.

elbow: **out at elbow**: 2.1.59: (a) ragged; (b) discomfited.

eld: **palsied eld**: old people afflicted with tremors and paralysis.

enforce them: 5.1.270: thrust them as evidence.

enmew: 3.1.91: (a) confine; (b) enew: force into water, suppress.

enshield: shielded, screened.

entertain: 3.1.74: maintain.

entertainment: 3.2.198: acceptance.

envy: malice.

escape of wit: witty falsehood.

essence: 2.2.126: spirit, soul.

estimation: esteem, repute.

events: **to his events**: to the outcome of his actions.

evils: 2.2.180: (a) filth; (b) privies; (c) vices; (d) emissions.

exeunt: they go out.

exit: he or she goes out.

facing: 3.2.10: (a) ornamented frontage; (b) effrontery.

fact: 4.2.130; 5.1.438: crime.

fall: 2.1.6: let fall.

fallow: arable land.

familiar: 1.4.31: habitual.

fast: 4.2.61: firmly; **fast my wife**: 1.2.135: (a) firmly my wife; (b) my wife by 'hand-fasting' (secular marriage).

favour: (i: 4.2.28–9: a) permission; (b) face; (ii: 4.2.166:) face.

fear: 2.1.2: frighten.

fedary: accomplice.

feelingly: 1.2.32–3: (a) impressively; (b) painfully.

fewness: briefly.

fie (interj.): foul, shame.

file (noun): number of people.

fine (noun): 2.2.45: penalty.

fine (vb.): 2.2.45; 3.1.117: punish.

finis (Latin): the end.

fitted: prepared.

flaw: 2.3.11: (a) fault; (b) gust of passion.

fleshmonger: pimp.

flourish: 4.1.76: vindicate.

foison: abundance.

fond: (i. 2.2.155:) trivial; (ii: 1.3.23; 2.2.195:) infatuated, doting; (iii: 5.1.109:) foolish.

fool: 3.1.11: dupe.

foppery: 1.2.122: folly.

forbear: 4.3.118: stop.

force: 3.1.112: enforce.

forfeits: (i: 5.1.323; 5.1.527:) penalties.

fork (noun): forked tongue.

forswear: 3.2.155: formally deny.

forsworn: 4.1.2; 5.1.39: false.

forted: fortified.

frame (noun): 5.1.63: structure.

frame (vb.): 3.1.253: prepare.

frankly: 3.1.107: freely.

free: (i: 1.1.77:) frank; (ii: 1.2.38:) healthy; (iii: 4.3.85:) willing; (iv: 5.1.392:) generous.

French crown: 1.2.46: (a) French gold coin; (b) bald head caused by syphilis.

French velvet: for a French velvet: 1.2.31–2: (a) as (fine) French velvet; (b) as a symptom of venereal disease.

fretting: 4.3.140: (a) corrosive; (b) agitated.

furred gown: garb associated with usurers.

gall: 3.2.175: rancour.

geld: castrate.

generous: 4.6.13: noble.

ghostly: (i: 4.3.43:) spiritual; (5.1.130: a) spiritual; (b) phantom, unreal.

giglets: whores.

glance: 5.1.311: turn.

glassy essence: 2.2.126: (a) invisible soul; (b) fragile life.

glimpse: 1.2.146: flash, glitter.

gnarlèd: knotted.

Goodman: Mister.

go to: 2.1.57: get on with it.

grace: (i: 1.2.17:) meal-time prayer of thanks; (ii: 1.2.23, 25:) divine blessing; (iii: 1.4.69; 3.1.183; 4.4.31:) God-given virtue; **moving graces**: 2.2.41: the gift of persuasion; **your Grace**: you, gracious lord.

graciously: 2.4.76: by divine grace.

gradation: **cold gradation**: calculated steps.

grange: isolated farm-house.

gratulate: 5.1.536: (a) gratifying; (b) rewarding.

gravel (adj.): stony.

guards: 3.1.98: ornamental borders.

guess: **I guess not**: I have no idea.

gyves: fetters.

habit: outfit.

Half-Can: Ale-Drinker.

Hallowmas: All Hallows' Feast:
  All Saints' Day, Nov.1st.

hand: bear in hand: deceive.

hanging look: 4.2.29:
  (a) gloomy expression;
  (b) hangman's face.

Hannibal: 2.1.164, 167:
  (a: error for) cannibal; (b:
  confusion with) Pompey.

happily: 4.2.90: perhaps.

heading: 2.1.219: beheading.

heavy: (i: 1.4.65:) harsh;
  (ii: 4.1.33:) deep.

helmed: steered.

hent: reached.

his: 4.2.105: its.

history: 1.1.28: life-story.

hold: 1.1.42: (a) take it;
  (b) don't argue.

Holiness: his Holiness: the
  Pope.

hollow: 1.2.50: eaten by
  venereal disease.

holy: 5.1.386: (a) dedicated;
  (b, error for) wholly.

home and home: to the utmost.

hooking: 2.4.177: catching
  like an angler.

hot-house: bath-house.

house: keep the house:
  3.2.68: (a) stay indoors;
  (b) manage the house.

husband: 3.2.68: (a) provident
  man; (b) married man.

husbandry: 1.4.44:
  (a) cultivation of soil;
  (b) marital sexuality.

ignomy: ignominy.

impartial: indifferent.

imputation: 5.1.424: censure.

inequality: 5.1.67:
  (a) difference in rank;
  (b) discrepancy.

informal: 5.1.240: (a)
  deranged; (b) disorderly.

information: 3.2.185: allegation.

injuries: 5.1.260: (a) wrongs;
  (b) slanders.

inward (noun): intimate friend.

jade: poor horse.

journal (adj.): daily.

Jove: 2.2.117: (a) chief Roman
  deity; (b) euphemism for God.

just: 3.1.67; 5.1.204: just so.

kennel: dog-kennel.

kersey: coarse English cloth.

knave: (i: 2.1.217:) whore's
  customer; (ii: 5.1.354:)
  rascal.

kneaded: (perhaps) kneadable.

know: (i: 5.1.190, 191, 425:)
  know carnally; (ii: 5.1.191:)
  be aware.

lapwing: 1.4.32: (a)
  deceptively-calling plover;
  (b) deceiver.

lay (adj.): secular.

league: about three miles.

lean upon: depend on.

leave: 4.2.5: cease.

leavened and prepared:
  carefully premeditated.

leiger: everlasting leiger:
  permanent ambassador.

leisure: attend your leisure:
  wait until you are ready.

levity: 5.1.225: promiscuity.

liberty: 1.2.114: license.

license: 3.2.190: licentiousness.

lief: gladly.

light (adj.): 5.1.283: promiscuous.

lightness: promiscuity.

like (adj.): 5.1.108: plausible.

likeness: 3.2.254: seeming, hypocrisy.

list: (i: 1.1.6:) limit; (ii: 1.2.30:) plain edging for cloth.

livery: **destined livery**: traditional appearance (of vulnerable womanhood).

long (vb.): 2.2.65: belong.

look: **hanging look**: 4.2.29: (a) gloomy expression; (b) hangman's face.

loose of question: freedom of conversation.

luxury: lechery.

maid: (i: 1.2.83: a) young fish: hence, child; (b) virgin, male or female; (c) girl; (ii: 5.1.22, 177:) virgin.

manifest: 5.1.303: clear; **manifested effect**: clear demonstration.

marry (interj., from 'by St. Mary'): indeed.

maw: stomach.

me: **come me**: 2.1.112: for my sake, come; **leave me**: 4.2.5: cease, for my sake.

mealed: stained.

means: 2.1.78–9: (a) agency; (b) agent.

medlar: **rotten medlar**: 4.3.164: (a) rotten medlar pear; (b) diseased whore.

meet (vb.): 4.1.18: keep an appointment.

meet (adj.): 2.3.30; 4.2.20: proper.

member: 5.1.241: person.

mercy: **cry you mercy**: beg your pardon.

mere: 3.1.30: pure; **merely**: 3.1.11: utterly; **but merely**: 5.1.458: nothing but; **upon his mere request**: solely because he asked.

mettle: (i: 1.1.48; 3.2.72: a) metal; (b) spirit, character.

minister: 5.1.119: angel.

miscarried: died accidentally.

Mitigation: Bringer of Sexual Relief.

moe: 1.3.48; 5.1.202: more in number; **moe thousand**: a thousand more.

mortal: **laugh mortal**: 2.2.129: (a) laugh to death; (b) laugh into human state.

mortality: (i: 1.1.44:) power to kill; (ii: 3.2.172:) mortal existence, human life.

Mother: 1.4.86: Mother Superior.

motion: (i: 3.1.122:) body; (ii: 5.1.542:) proposal; **motion ungenerative**: sexless puppet; **motions of the sense**: sensual impulses.

muffled: with face concealed.

Mum: I'm silent.

murtherer: murderer.

mutton: **eat mutton**: 3.2.168–9: (a) consume mutton; (b) use a whore.

myrtle: **soft myrtle**: shrub emblematic of love and vulnerable to coldness.

mystery: highly-skilled profession.

name: 1.2.157, 159: reputation.

nature: (i: 3.1.133:) a person's self; (ii: 3.1.137: a) natural affection; (b) Nature as judge.

naughty: wicked.

new-made: 2.2.85: (a) newly-created, prelapsarian; (b) regenerated by Christ's sacrifice.

nip youth i'th'head: forcefully curb young people.

notable: 5.1.271: notorious.

obstruction: 3.1.121: confinement.

omit: 4.3.67: disregard.

open room: public room.

opposite (noun): opponent.

organ: 1.1.20: instrument.

outward order: public ceremony.

owe: (i: 1.4.83:) grant; (ii: 2.4.124:) own.

parcel bawd: partly a pimp (and partly a barman).

part: 2.4.28: place.

passes (noun): 5.1.371: (a) trespasses, sins; (b) actions.

pavèd bed: tomb.

peach (vb.): 4.3.11: impeach, bring to trial as.

pelting (adj.): paltry.

pendent: hanging.

peradventure: by chance.

perdurably: eternally.

pérfect him withal: fully inform him of.

perfection: 3.1.258: completion.

pervert your course: misdirect you.

petition: 1.2.14: prayer.

petty: minor.

Philip and Jacob: the festival of Saints Philip and James, May 1st.

pick-lock: skeleton key.

piled: 1.2.31: (a) peeled, rendered bald by venereal disease; (b) with nap; **three-piled**: 1.2.30: (a) having richly-napped velvet; (b) thrice-peeled.

pitch (vb.): 2.2.180: (a) cast; (b) erect.

pith: essence.

pity of her life: a pity she should live.

place (noun): 1.2.151: office.

planchèd: made of boards or planks.

point: **to the point**: punctiliously.

Pompey the Great: Roman general.

pose (vb.): 2.4.50: ask.

powdered: 3.2.57: (a) fumigated with powders; (b) using face-powder.

practice: 5.1.111, 127, 243: plot, conspiracy.

precept: **in action all of precept**: with amply explanatory gestures.

precise: 2.1.53: (error for) precious, i.e. arrant.

pre-contract: formal betrothal.

pregnant: 2.1.23: (a) obvious; (b) cogent (*O.E.D.*).

pressing to death: using weights to suffocate a victim.

pretend: 3.1.225: allege.

prince: ruler, head of state.

probation: proof.

process: 5.1.96: account.

proclamation: 3.2.133: open declaration.

profanation: 2.1.54: (error for) veneration.

profess: 2.1.63: purport (to manage).

prolixious: protracted.

prone: 1.2.171: eager (*O.E.D.*).

propagation: 1.2.138: (a) increase; (b) generation.

proper: (i: 1.1.30:) exclusively; (ii: 1.2.118:) specific; (iii: 3.1.30; 5.1.310; 5.1.412:) very own; (iv: 5.1.114:) peculiar to.

proportion: (i: 1.2.21:) form; (ii: 5.1.222:) portion, dowry.

provincial: belonging to an ecclesiastical province.

provoke: 3.1.18: solicit.

Provost: prison governor.

punk: prostitute.

put: putting on: incitement, pressing forward; put to know: informed.

Pygmalion: sculptor of a statue which became a living woman.

qualify: 4.2.78: moderate.

quality: 2.1.57: profession.

quest: 4.1.61: (a) pursuit; (b) bark at game.

question: 2.4.89: argument; in question: involved in the matter.

quit: (i: 5.1.415, 513:) repay; (ii: 5.1.490:) pardon.

quite: 4.4.18: utterly.

rack (vb.): 4.1.64: distort, tear.

ravin down: gulp down.

raze: erase, blot out.

razure of oblivion: obliteration by forgetfulness.

rebate (vb.): blunt, dull.

refelled: repelled.

relish (vb.): enjoy.

remit: cancel.

remonstrance: demonstration.

remorse: pity, compassion.

removed: 1.3.8: secluded.

report: blistered her report: sullied her reputation.

reprieve: 2.4.38: time before death.

reprobate: hardened sinner.

requital: 2.1.225; 5.1.8: reward.

resolve: 3.1.190; 4.2.199: convince.

resort: house of resort: brothel.

respected: 2.1.152–65: (error for) suspected.

rest (vb.): 2.3.37: remain.

restrainèd: 2.4.47: forbidden, prohibited.

retort: 5.1.303: (a) turn away; (b) reject (*O.E.D.*).

reveal: 5.1.29: explain.

rheum: excess of fluid, e.g. catarrh.

riotous youth: youthful wildness.

rude: 3.2.32; 4.3.75: crude, rough.

salt (adj.): salacious.

sapego: serpigo: spreading skin-disease.

saucy: 2.4.44; 5.1.139: lascivious.

scaled: 3.1.252: weighed up, assessed.

scape: 3.2.173: escape.

sciatica: 1.2.53: neuralgia of hip and thigh, here deemed a symptom of venereal disease.

science: knowledge.

scope: (i: 1.1.64; 3.1.69:) room to move; (ii: 1.2.116; 1.3.35:) license, liberty; (iii: 5.1.238:) whole extent.

scruple: (i: 1.1.37: a) apothecary's 20-grain weight; (b) tiny amount; (ii: 1.1.64:) tiny doubt.

scurvy (adj.): low, vile.

sealed in approbation: officially sealed to guarantee authenticity.

sea-maid: mermaid.

seared: arid.

season: **of season**: in season.

sect: class, rank.

security: 3.2.212: complacency. See: Vatican.

seedness: sowing.

seeming: (i: 2.4.15, 151:) appearance; (ii: 2.4.151:) hypocrisy.

sense: (i: 1.4.59:) sexual desire; (ii: 1.4.65:) meaning; (iii:

2.2.148: a) sound sense; (b) sexual desire; (iv: 4.4.27:) urges; **betray our sense**: 2.2.177: (a) elicit our lust; (b) subvert our good sense.

sensible: 3.1.122: sensitive, able to feel.

sequent: subsequent.

sere: stale.

settled: 3.1.90: composed.

sheep-biting: 5.1.355: (a) wolfish; (b) currish.

shield (vb.): (i: 3.1.143:) forbid; (ii: 5.1.122:) protect.

shore: 3.2.234: limit.

shrift: **present shrift**: prompt hearing of confession.

shy: 3.2.123; 5.1.56: reserved.

sickles: shekels: coins.

siege: throne.

Signor (It.): Mister.

sinew: **portion and sinew**: allocation and mainstay.

sinister: 3.2.226: unjust.

skin (vb.): cover superficially.

slander: **do in slander**: (possibly) provoke slander.

smack of: share in.

snatch (noun): quip, quibble.

snow-broth: melted snow.

something: (i: 1.1.61:) some distance; (ii: 3.2.93:) somewhat.

sort: 4.4.15: rank.

soul: **special soul**: intense consideration.

sound (adj.): 1.2.48–50: (a) healthy; (b) resounding.

spared: 2.2.17: dispensed with.

splay: spay: excise ovaries.

spleen: 2.2.128: source of mirth (as well as wrath).

stagger: **I stagger in**: I am uncertain.

stand: 4.6.10: vantage-point.

starkly: stiffly.

Starve-Lackey: Mean-Master.

stay upon: wait for.

stead: **stead me**: help me; **stead up**: fulfil as proxy.

stew: 5.1.320: (a) stew-pot; (b) brothel.

still: 2.1.262; 5.1.478: always.

sting: 1.4.59: impulse.

stir my temper: excite me.

stock-fish: dried fish.

stone: 2.2.156: precious stone, jewel.

story: 1.4.30: dupe, butt.

strait: strict; **straitness**: strictness.

stricture: strictness, severity.

strife: 3.2.217: endeavour.

stroke and line: exact course.

stuck: 4.1.60: fastened.

subject: **general subject to**: common people who are subjects of.

suborned: procured for a plot.

success: 1.4.89: result.

sue: (i: 1.4.80; 2.4.164:) plead; (ii: 3.1.42, 173:) seek.

sufficiency: competence.

supposed: 2.1.147: (error for) deposed.

surfeit: gluttony; **surfeiting**: glutted, sated.

sweat (noun): 1.2.73: (a) febrile disease; (b) sweating-treatment for venereal diseases.

swinged: thrashed.

tainted: diseased.

tapster: barman, waiter.

tax: (i: 2.4.78:) denigrate; (ii: 5.1.312:) charge.

temporal: worldly.

temporary: temporal.

tender: 2.4.181: (a) pay; (b) extend.

tenor: substance, gist.

terms: 1.1.10: vocabulary.

thick-ribbèd: strongly-ridged.

This' a: 5.1.135: This is a.

three pence: small sum of money; **give you three pence again**: give you change for your payment.

Three-Pile: Rich-Velvet.

thrilling: chilling, piercingly cold.

thus, and thus: more of the same.

tickle (adv.): insecurely.

tick-tack: 1.2.178: (a) kind of backgammon; (b) coitus.

tilth: tillage.

time: **in good time**: (i: 3.1.180:) well and good; (ii: 5.1.288:) opportunely.

tithe: rent paid in crops.

tongue (vb.): denounce.

to't: (i: 2.1.215:) fornicate; (ii: 3.2.90:) to correction; (iii: 4.3.148:) to lechery.

touch (noun): 5.1.145: sexual contact.

touched: 5.1.239: irritated.

towze: rip.

trade (noun): 3.1.151: career.

travail: travel.

traveller: 4.2.62: labourer.

trick: (i: 2.2.127:) prank; (ii: 3.1.116:) sexual act; (iii: 3.2.50:) particular habit or custom; (iv: 3.2.87:) caprice; (v: 5.1.512: a) prank; (b) whim; (c) habit.

trot (noun): (contemptuous term for) old person.

trumpet: trumpeter.

tub: 3.2.55: tub for treating venereal disease.

tun-dish: funnel.

tune: 3.2.47: mood.

turn: 4.2.54: (a) favour; (b) hanging.

unfold: 1.1.3: explain.

unfolding star: Morning Star (Venus).

ungenitured: sexless.

unhappy: unfortunate.

unkindness: 2.4.167: lack of natural feeling.

unmeet: unfit.

unpitied: pitiless.

unpregnant: stupid.

unshape: discompose.

unshunned: inevitable.

unskilfully: 3.2.136: ignorantly.

untrussing: uncovering the penis.

unwedgeable: too strong to be split by wedges.

unweighing: thoughtless.

use: (i: 1.1.40: a) interest; (b) application; (ii: 3.2.119) custom; **use their abuses**: indulge their vices.

vail your regard: look down.

vain: **for vain**: 2.4.12: (a) in vain; (b) for its vanity; (c) as a vane.

vantage: **have such vantage on**: be so well located near.

varlet: villain.

vastidity: immensity.

very (adj.): 1.4.53: true.

viewless: invisible.

vouch (noun): assertion.

vouch (vb.): assert.

vouchsafe: allow.

vulgarly: publicly.

wait on: attend.

wanton: 1.4.59: (a) frisky, unruly; (b) lascivious.

ward: cell.

warp: deviate; **warpèd**: crooked.

warrant (noun): writ of arrest.

warrant (vb.): assure.

warranted: genuine, confirmed.

wear (noun): 3.2.70: fashion.

weary: wearisome, tedious.

weight: **pay down by weight**: pay promptly and fully.

wend: depart, go.

widow (vb.): 5.1.428: settle an estate on a widow.

wilderness: wildness.

woodman: woman-hunter.

worm: snake.

worth (noun): (i: 1.1.8:) standing, authority; (ii: 5.1.505:) personal qualities.

worth (vb.): 5.1.505: are worthy of.

wot: know.

wracked: wrecked.

yare: brisk, eager.